# Future Army Bandwidth Needs and Capabilities

LELAND JOE
ISAAC PORCHE III

Prepared for the United States Army

ARROYO CENTER

The research described in this report was sponsored by the United States Army under Contract No. DASW01-01-C-0003.

ISBN 0-8330-3545-2

The RAND Corporation is a nonprofit research organization providing objective analysis and effective solutions that address the challenges facing the public and private sectors around the world. RAND's publications do not necessarily reflect the opinions of its research clients and sponsors.

**RAND**® is a registered trademark.

Published 2004 by the RAND Corporation
1700 Main Street, P.O. Box 2138, Santa Monica, CA 90407-2138
1200 South Hayes Street, Arlington, VA 22202-5050
201 North Craig Street, Suite 202, Pittsburgh, PA 15213-1516
RAND URL: http://www.rand.org/
To order RAND documents or to obtain additional information, contact
Distribution Services: Telephone: (310) 451-7002;
Fax: (310) 451-6915; Email: order@rand.org

# Preface

This report presents the results for a RAND Arroyo Center project, "Future Army Bandwidth Needs." The research documented here addresses the problems of designing the Army's future communications network to meet competing demands at a time of rapidly changing user needs and technologies. The research will interest the combat development, research and development, and acquisition communities.

This project was sponsored by the G-6 and CIO, Headquarters Department of the Army, and was conducted within RAND Arroyo Center's Force Development and Technology Program. RAND Arroyo Center, part of the RAND Corporation, is a federally funded research and development center sponsored by the United States Army.

For more information on RAND Arroyo Center, contact the Director of Operations (telephone 310-393-0411, extension 6419; FAX 310-451-6952; e-mail Marcy_Agmon@rand.org), or visit Arroyo's web site at http://www.rand.org/ard/.

# The RAND Corporation Quality Assurance Process

Peer review is an integral part of all RAND research projects. Prior to publication, this document, as with all documents in the RAND monograph series, was subject to a quality assurance process to ensure that the research meets several standards, including the following: The problem is well formulated; the research approach is well designed and well executed; the data and assumptions are sound; the findings are useful and advance knowledge; the implications and recommendations follow logically from the findings and are explained thoroughly; the documentation is accurate, understandable, cogent, and temperate in tone; the research demonstrates understanding of related previous studies; and the research is relevant, objective, independent, and balanced. Peer review is conducted by research professionals who were not members of the project team.

RAND routinely reviews and refines its quality assurance process and also conducts periodic external and internal reviews of the quality of its body of work. For additional details regarding the RAND quality assurance process, visit http://www.rand.org/standards/.

# Contents

# Figures

# Tables

# Summary

Across the services, there is an increasing demand for communications capacity. For the U.S. Army, this is a result of the Army's transition to a new force structure that will be knowledge-based[1] and network-centric.[2] Since bandwidth facilitates communications capacity, bandwidth has become increasingly critical. To the user, high bandwidth is useful because it supports increased capacity, high-volume data exchange, short delays, and high assurance of connectivity. New technologies, commercial and military, will continue to increase available bandwidth and hence the communications capacity available to users. Based on specified requirements and proposed technologies and architectures for the future force, the capacity of communications systems planned to support the new force structure will continue to fall short of the required demand.

With unlimited spectrum and unlimited budget, the Army could resolve its bandwidth issues. But these are unrealistic assumptions. Certainly, demand reduction can help close the gap between the requirements and availability of network capacity. However, it is not clear how much demand reduction is possible while retaining the information dominance that is critical for the future force. Demand reduction will need to be coupled with technology investments (e.g., satellites, UAVs, directional antennas, more radios). A number of

---

[1] Casper et al. (1996).

[2] Cebrowski and Garstka (1998).

technologies and concepts are being developed to enhance spectral efficiency, thus allowing the Army to make the best use of the available spectrum. Gaps between the supply and demand of capacity, both now and in the future, will have to be addressed by constantly reassessing demand for capacity and developing technologies that increase the supply.

It is important to note that bandwidth is not the only issue with regard to networked communication. Among the other critical issues are communications-on-the-move (not widely possible in Operation Iraqi Freedom) and interoperability. The Joint Tactical Radio System will be required to address these two issues.

Although the Army can take advantage of commercially developed technologies, the Army's operational situation differs fundamentally from that of industry. Currently, the Army differs from commercial industry in its approach to user and communications infrastructure mobility, information assurance (i.e., secure communication), and interoperability. It is not clear that the commercial world will be the source of all of the technology solutions. Department of Defense (DoD) funded initiatives are likely to be critical to the development of the key technologies.

Recent RAND Arroyo Center research analyzed how the Army uses bandwidth. As a result, this report describes a number of specific steps that can be taken to address the gap. They are listed below in order of priority, where priority is assigned to the steps that are likely to lead to the largest gains, based on our assessment.

## Reassess Information Demands and Needs

The Army must perform experiments to understand what drives "real-world" information demands. There exists only a scant amount of data on the details of real-world demands and there has been little analysis of the necessity and the value of proposed information flows at each of the various echelons. Furthermore, the Army must reassess the necessity of these information requests. More experimentation is needed to test how various information demands contribute to mission success.

## Change Application Structure

Applications determine the volume and timing of a large part of information flow. Adjusting applications demands, such as by compression, can decrease bandwidth requirements by orders of magnitude. Minimizing the need to transmit raw sensor data will be beneficial, especially if local fusion is feasible. However, explicit performance assessments must be conducted to maintain quality with respect to data fusion and compression.

## Manage Operational Demands to Meet Needs

Information traffic patterns exhibit differing needs for different priority users. Changing information needs require a dynamic network management approach to prioritize and smooth flow through the network. This has already been explicitly recommended in an Operation Iraqi Freedom after action report.[3]

## Increase Efficiency of Network Routing

Army communications are increasingly network based and must be addressed from a network perspective. The Army Communications-Electronics Command (CECOM), the Defense Advanced Research Projects Agency (DARPA), and commercial industry are attempting to increase capacity through more efficient routing through networks.

---

[3] Shaaber, Hedberg, and Wesson (2003) call for the "ability to manage bandwidth usage dynamically at the discretion of the commander [to allocate bandwidth] commensurate with operational priorities."

These techniques take advantage of knowledge of the network state to improve routing efficiency.

## Increase Capacities of Links

Both CECOM and DARPA (e.g., in their FCS Communications and Next-Generation Communications programs) are working to increase link capacities by using higher frequencies and directional antennas. Theoretical assessments by Yi, Pei, and Kalyanaraman (2003) show that the capacity-multiplying effect of directional antennas over today's nondirectional (omnidirectional) antennas could be as high as one to two orders of magnitude, depending on the technology used. These are better results than what has been seen in simulation of various types of directional systems. Clearly, the opportunity for improvement exists, and more development is needed to fully realize the benefits of this concept. If directional antenna systems can be developed to their full potential, they could help ameliorate the inherent capacity limitations of large numbers of radios sharing a frequency channel.

Today's fixed, limited frequency allocation of available spectrum creates a hard limit on the amount of capacity, especially for ground vehicles on the move. Commercial demands in the United States, Europe, and elsewhere are squeezing the available spectrum for use by the U.S. military and its allies.[4] By one estimate, there may be as little as 55 MHz available[5] today for the Army; this could translate into 50 to 100 Mbps capacity for a given area of operation, at best. (Such

---

[4] Quoting: "high-tech companies are lobbying to block the recent DOD proposal [to open up the 5,150 to 5,720] megahertz band to accommodate the burgeoning industry." *Inside the Pentagon*, "DoD Battles Industry on Spectrum Wanted for Wireless Networking," December 2002.

[5] This is when given only the JTRS threshold operating frequencies, which are between 2 Mhz and 2 Ghz, when considering availability for the Future Combat Systems (FCS) communication network. U.S. Army, "FCS WNW Spectrum Requirement" white paper, December 6, 2002.

limited spectrum access in CONUS also prohibits the "train as you fight" notion.) The lower end of this range may not be sufficient to accommodate one brigade-sized unit's situational awareness needs.[6]

Spectral reuse is key to achieving as much capacity as possible. Directional antennas facilitate reuse even with fixed frequency/spectral allocations. Fully dynamic spectrum management could facilitate even greater reuse of the spectrum by obviating the need for static channel/frequency assignments. DARPA is developing technologies to enable dynamic access to radio frequency spectrum. This is an important technology concept that needs to continue development.

## Overall Assessment and Recommendations

Bandwidth is a limited resource that needs to be managed. New technologies will greatly increase capacity, but unchecked user demands will probably keep pace and exceed available capacities. No single technique will solve the problem. There are no silver bullets.

The challenge is to meet the right users' needs at the right time. To achieve this, it is recommended the Army do the following. First, bandwidth needs to be treated as an operational resource to be allocated by commanders and staffs. Second, the Army should continue to pursue all technologies that could provide benefit. Technology development should be synchronized through a single cognizant agency for efficiency and coordination. This includes not only communications systems but also systems-of-systems to reduce demands and create an overall information architecture. Third, the Army should develop and refine assessment tools; better assessment tools are needed to make complex tradeoffs. Last, the Army needs to make a partner of DoD to avoid unnecessary redirection and to take advantage of DoD-wide capabilities. This is especially important with respect to the

---

[6] Assuming an average situational awareness (SA) data rate of 64 kilobits per second per vehicle/node and a 1,000+ node brigade.

DoD efforts to maintain and perhaps acquire new spectral allocations.

# Acknowledgments

The authors would like to thank Lewis Saunders, COL Philip Vermeer, LTG Peter Couviello, and LTG Steven Boutelle of the Office of the Chief Information officer, G-6, U.S. Army, for their assistance in and support for this research project.

LTC Larry Gordon made contributions to this report. He provided important guidance and direction as well as access to data.

We are indebted to our RAND Corporation colleagues, including Jerry Sollinger, Ken Horn, and Tom McNaugher, who provided important advice and counsel during the course of this study. Lou Moore and Ed Balkovich served as the technical reviewers of this report.

The RAND support staff is what keeps the work moving; we would like to especially thank Stephanie Sutton for her many contributions. We, of course, remain responsible for the observations and judgments contained in this report.

# Glossary

| | |
|---|---|
| 1G | First Generation Mobile Phone Technology |
| 2G | Second Generation Mobile Phone Technology |
| 3G | Third Generation Mobile Phone Technology |
| 4G | Fourth Generation Mobile Phone Technology |
| ACT | Airspace Control Team |
| ADPCM | Adaptive Differential Pulse Code Modulation |
| AJ | Anti-jamming |
| AMSAA | Army Materiel Systems Analysis Activity |
| AODV | Ad hoc On-Demand Distance Vector |
| AP | Access Point |
| ARL | Army Research Laboratory |
| ARO | Army Research Office |
| ASD (NII) | Assistant Secretary of Defense for Networks and Information Integration (formerly ASD/C3I) |
| ASD/C3I | Assistant Secretary of Defense for Command, Control, Communications, and Intelligence |
| ATM | Asynchronous Transfer Mode |
| bps | Bits per second |
| C2 | Command and Control |
| C3I | Command, Control, Communications, and Intelligence |

| | |
|---|---|
| C4ISR | Command, Control, Communications, Computers, Intelligence, Surveillance, and Reconnaissance |
| CBRP | Cluster Based Routing Protocol |
| CDMA | Code Division Multiple Access |
| CECOM | (U.S. Army) Communications-Electronics Command |
| CEDAR | Core Extraction Distributed Ad Hoc Routing |
| CERDEC | CECOM Research, Development, and Engineering Center |
| COTS | Commercial-off-the-Shelf |
| CSMA/CA | Carrier Sense Multiple Access/Collision Avoidance |
| CTS | Clear to Send |
| DARPA | Defense Advanced Research Projects Agency |
| DAWE | Division Advanced Warfighting Experiment |
| DISN | Defense Integrated Systems Network |
| DMS | Defense Message System |
| DMTD | Digital Message Transfer Device |
| DoD | Department of Defense |
| DSDV | Destination Sequence Distance Vector |
| DSR | Dynamic Source Routing |
| DSSS | Direct Sequence Spread Spectrum |
| EHF | Extremely High Frequency |
| EPLRS | Enhanced Position Location Reporting System |
| FADAC | Field Artillery Digital Automatic Computer |
| FBCB2 | Force (XXI) Battle Command Brigade and Below Systems |
| FCS | Future Combat Systems |
| FH-CDMA | Frequency Hopping Code Division Multiple Access |
| FHSS | Frequency Hopping Spread Spectrum |
| FLIRS | Forward Looking Infrared System |
| FM | Frequency Modulation |

| | |
|---|---|
| Gbps | Gigabits per second |
| GBS | Global Broadcast System |
| GCCS | Global Command and Control System |
| GHz | Gigahertz |
| GIG | Global Information Grid |
| GPS | Global Positioning System |
| GSM | Global Systems for Mobile Communication |
| HCLOS | High-Capacity Line of Sight |
| HF | High Frequency |
| Hz | Hertz |
| IEEE | Institute for Electrical and Electronic Engineers |
| ISM | Industrial, Scientific, and Medical |
| ISO | International Standards Organization |
| ISYSCON | Integrated System Control |
| JTRS | Joint Tactical Radio System |
| LAM | Loitering Attack Missile |
| LAN | Local Area Network |
| LOS | Line of Sight |
| LPD | Low Probability of Detection |
| LPI | Low Probability of Intercept |
| LW | Land Warrior |
| MANET | Mobile Ad Hoc Network |
| Mbps | Megabits per second |
| MCM | Multicarrier Modulation |
| MHz | Megahertz |
| MOSAIC | Multifunctional On-the-Move Secure Adaptive Integrated Communications |
| MSE | Mobile Subscriber Equipment |
| MSRT | Mobile Subscriber Radio Terminal |

| NETEX | Networking in Extreme Environments |
| NSSA | National Security Space Architect |
| NTDR | Near-Term Digital Radio |
| ODMA | Orthogonal Division Multiple Access |
| OEF | Operation Enduring Freedom |
| OFDM | Orthogonal Frequency Division Multiplexing |
| OIF | Operation Iraqi Freedom |
| OLSR | Optimized Link State Routing Protocol |
| ORD | Operational Requirements Document |
| PAM | Precision Attack Missile |
| PBX | Private Branch Exchange |
| PDC | Personal Digital Cellular or Personal Digital Communication |
| PN | Pseudo Noise |
| QoS | Quality of Service |
| RDMAR | Relative Distance Micro-Discovery Ad hoc Routing |
| RF | Radio Frequency |
| RTS | Request to Send |
| SA | Situational Awareness |
| SBCT | Stryker Brigade Combat Team |
| SHF | Super High Frequency |
| SINCGARS | Single-Channel Ground and Airborne Radio System |
| SMART-T | Secure Mobile Anti-Jam Reliable Tactical-Terminal |
| SS | Spread Spectrum |
| STAR | Source Tree Adaptive Routing |
| SUO SAS | Small Unit Operations Situation Awareness System |
| SUV | Sports Utility Vehicle |
| TCA | Transformational Communication Architecture |
| TCP | Transmission Control Protocol or Transfer Control Protocol |

| | |
|---|---|
| TDMA | Time Division Multiple Access |
| THOR | Tera Hertz Operational Reachback |
| THSDN | Tactical High Speed Data Network |
| TORA | Temporally Ordered Routing Algorithm |
| TRAC | Training and Doctrine Command Analysis Center |
| UAV | Unmanned Aerial Vehicle |
| UDAAN | Utilizing Directional Antennas for Ad hoc Networking |
| UGS | Unattended Ground Sensors |
| UHF | Ultra High Frequency |
| VAA | Vehicle Amplifier/Adapter Assembly |
| VHF | Very High Frequency |
| WLAN | Wireless Local Area Network |
| ZRP | Zone Routing Protocol |

# CHAPTER ONE

# Introduction

## Background

The Army is moving toward network-based communications in which all users (sensors, shooters, commanders, etc.) are interconnected as part of an information grid (see Figure 1.1). The information grid is a network of networks supporting voice, video, and data transmissions. It supports more than just the passing of targeting information through sensor-to-shooter loops; such a grid also provides, for example, real-time collaboration and dynamic planning. From a communications standpoint, a key measure of a network is its capacity to transmit and receive information. In the Army, the term "bandwidth" is synonymous with the capacity of its communication networks.

The Army's networked approach has both technical and operational advantages. It offers technical advantages in that networked communications effectively extend the range of communications, since any user in a network can connect to any other user through the network. Operationally, sensors, command and control units, and shooters are interconnected to maximize their effectiveness.

Networking, especially that based on Internet protocols, can also take advantage of commercially developed software applications for information sharing and collaboration. The remainder of this section describes basic definitions of links, networks, link capacity, network capacity, and bandwidth.

**Figure 1.1**
**Information Grid Connects the Various Distributed**
**Sensors and Shooters Across the Battlespace**

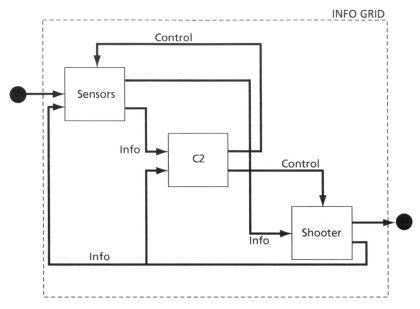

RAND *MG156-1.1*

SOURCE: Cebrowski and Garstka (1998).

## Link Capacity

Networks are made up of nodes, which in the context of the military are command vehicles, soldiers, sensors, and other users and producers of information. Nodes are said to be connected (or linked) if they can exchange information. Such links are facilitated using radios, satellite terminals, and other communication devices. The capacity of a link is quantified in terms of the maximum rate of information flow on the network, i.e., the maximum number of bits that can be transmitted per second. Link capacity is a function of the bandwidth (i.e., frequencies spanned) as indicated by Shannon's equation as follows:

$$C = W \cdot \log_2(1 + SNR),$$

where

C = capacity, bits/sec,
W = bandwidth, Hz,
SNR = signal to noise ratio.

This equation assumes (1) an Additive White Gaussian Noise (AWGN) channel and (2) a single-input single-output (SISO) system.

It is important to note that if a fixed amount of bandwidth is allocated for an application, it has a finite amount of capacity. In other words, bandwidth and link capacity are inextricably linked (and, thus, so are spectrum allocation and capacity). Note that the two terms "bandwidth" and "capacity" are often used interchangeably despite the fact that they differ depending on the context.

The term spectrum also refers to a range (or band) of frequencies measured in Hertz (Hz). Spectral efficiency is a measure that relates the data rates possible for a given span of frequencies. It is measured in bits per second per Hertz. Spectral efficiency depends on the communication technologies involved and could be lower or greater than one. The spectral efficiencies of various Army radios are compared in Chapter Two.

In general, higher frequencies and larger frequency bands facilitate higher capacities. Note that secure communication (e.g., requirements of low probability of detection, low probability of intercept, and/or anti-jam) can have a lower spectral efficiency.

## Network Capacity

The capacity of a network, as a whole, differs from the capacity of individual links within that network. The capacity of a network is determined by the capacities of the links and is also expressed in bits per second. Total network capacity for a fixed wired network is often tabulated as the sum of link capacities between network nodes. As an example, consider Figure 1.2, which is a two-node network with three links between the nodes; if the capacity of each link is 1 Mbps,

**Figure 1.2**
**A Simple Network**

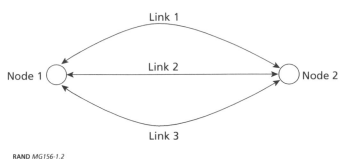

RAND *MG156-1.2*

network capacity could be as high as 3 Mbps if it is assumed that the transmissions can occur simultaneously. Note that the capacity of a network does not directly imply the capacity of any individual links. Thus, specifications of network capacity (or bandwidth) as a single number cannot be used in isolation to assess actual data rates across the links and among a network's nodes.[1]

## Factors Affecting Network Capacity

The capacity of a wireless communication link (or channel) increases with the channel bandwidth, as shown in Shannon's equation. There are a number of terrain-specific factors that can enhance or degrade wireless capacity for a given spectral allocation. These include (1) the distance between node pairs and (2) line of sight between node pairs (i.e., whether or not node pairs are within each other's line of sight).

In an ideal case, there exists a short transmission distance and clear line of sight between node pairs that are communicating. When this is not the case, messages will have to be forwarded between intermediary nodes. Such "forward hopping" is far less efficient than direct connections. Figure 1.3 shows analysis from Holland and

---

[1] Rather, network capacity requirements have to be specified within a specific network structure. A listing of the capacity between major nodes of a network is needed to understand capacity requirements and constraints. For the Army, this translates into understanding the data rates between and among the various echelons.

**Figure 1.3**
**Throughput as a Function of "Hops" Using Commercial Standards/Protocols**

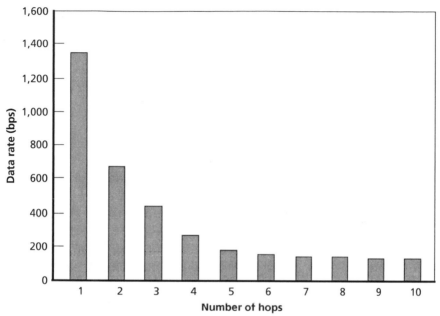

RAND *MG15G-1.3*

Vaidya (1999) that assumes a network of 2 Mbps wireless radio transmitters using the transmission control protocol (TCP).[2] Their observations show how network capacity diminishes exponentially based on the amount of hopping. Furthermore, these simulation results are in line with Gupta and Kumar's (1999) theoretical findings regarding network scalability with omnidirectional antennas, which suggest a similar decline based on just the numbers of nodes; simply put: the larger the network, the more hopping required[3] and thus the less overall capacity. As the network grows, more hops are needed to

---

[2] A number of protocols have been proposed that would produce better results in a wireless environment than TCP (see Appendix B).

[3] Overhead (or nondata) messages that are required to be exchanged in order to maintain a network's ability to pass messages also may have to hop, and such overhead increases with network size.

connect distributed nodes, which could result in the significant degrading of network capacity for certain types of networks. For example, a 100-node network of 2 Mbps radios,[4] all sharing a communication channel, could have the capacity that is one-tenth $(1/\sqrt{100})$ that peak rate. Simulation results by others bear this out.[5]

Network scale significantly affects capacity. Commercial, static, and "flat" wireless networks may have significant scaling limitations.[6] Figure 1.4 shows three results. The theoretical results[7] of Gupta and Kumar (1999) are used to plot[8] how per-node capacity (in bits per second) decreases with the size of the network. Experimental results[9] from Gupta, Gray, and Kumar (2001) are also shown and suggest that the potential decrease in throughput is even worse than what theory predicts. This suggests that commercial hardware for mobile ad hoc networks could benefit from improved hardware and protocols. Another curve is shown to represent, in a modest fashion, the potential improvements that result from using directional antennas.

---

[4] The JTRS Cluster 1 radio has a user throughput specification of 2 Mbps as a threshold value, according to the JTRS WNW Functional Description Document accessed at http://www.herbb.hanscom.af.mil/tbbs/R459/ATT5_WNW_FDD.pdf.

[5] Li et al. (2001) highlighted an interesting result in citing the simulation work of Das, Perkins, and Royer (2000). Quoting: "in a simulated network of 100 nodes, each with 2 Mbps radio, the throughput available to each node is on the order of a few kilobits per second." Using GloMoSim, Li et al. simulate 1,000 nodes over a 3.2-km-square field in which the nodes are divided into 36 groups and nodes have transmission range of .175 km. As shown in Figure 1.4, Gupta, Gray, and Kumar (2001) report experiments in which per-node throughput decays like $c/n^{1.68}$.

[6] Mobility can be one of the factors that constrain the capacity of these types of networks because it can induce the necessity of additional overhead message traffic.

[7] Key assumptions for their result: a notional network of randomly placed nodes each capable of transmitting 2.0 Mbps using omnidirectional antennas.

[8] The figure uses $W/\sqrt{n * \log(n)}$ as capacity to form the plot that represents theoretical results, where W = 2.0 Mbps.

[9] Gupta, Gray, and Kumar (2001) set up experiments with IBM laptops that used IEEE standard 802.11 compliant WaveLAN Turbo Bronze PCMIA cards that supported 2 Mbps transmission rates.

**Figure 1.4**
**Capacity of a (Random Access) Network Decreases with Size**

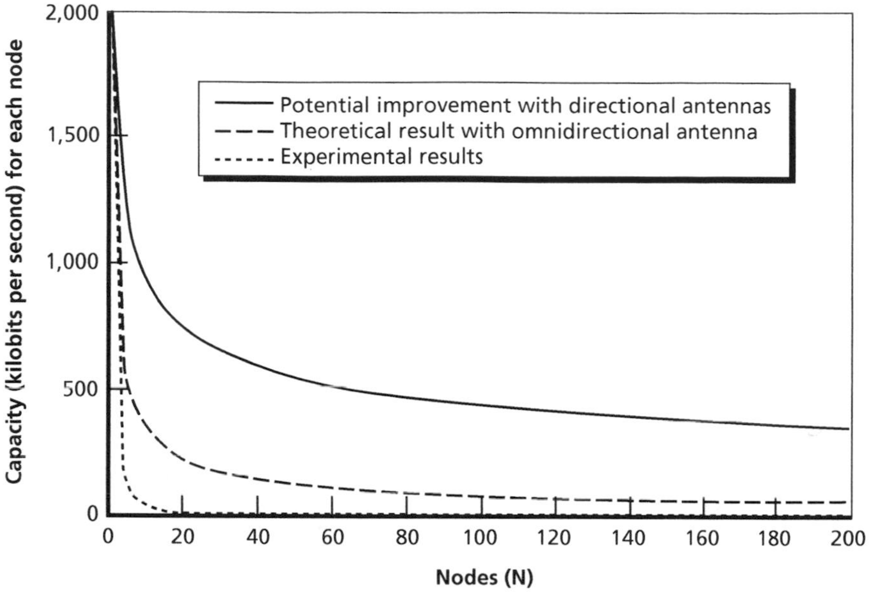

RAND MG156-1.4

## Performance Measures

It is important to note that bandwidth and capacity are not the only measures of communications performance that have to be considered. Other important measures are timeliness, accuracy, efficiency, latency, throughput, and reliability. In addition, a communications network must support user needs for mobility and reconfigurability, information assurance, and interoperability. Quality of service (QoS), where the measures listed above can be appropriated or guaranteed based on the priority (importance) of the message, is also critical. These user requirements result in communications design tradeoffs, not all of which are mutually compatible.

A specific type of network, mobile ad hoc networks (MANETs), will be required for future forces. Quoting: "To survive under battlefield conditions, warfighters and their mobile platforms must be able to move about freely without any restrictions imposed by wireless communication devices . . . the military cannot rely on access to a fixed, preplaced communications infrastructure" (Freebersyser and Leiner (2001) quoted in Perkins (2001), pp. 30–31). By definition, MANETs must provide redundant connectivity to compensate for the loss of individual nodes and links.

### Enhancing Network Capacity

The constraints on capacity described do not reflect advanced technologies that could ease these constraints, such as directional antennas, which by their nature have better range and thus ameliorate the need to forward/hop messages to some degree. In addition, a hierarchical scheme can be implemented that employs "backbone" nodes to reduce the volume of message hopping from a source to a destination. There are other "smart" routing schemes (aside from TCP) designed to minimize the impact of communication overhead and minimize the necessity of message hopping in a wireless environment. In other words, the outlook on the impact of network size on capacity is perhaps less bleak than what Figure 1.4 suggests when new technologies and concepts are considered.

The Stryker Brigade Combat Team (SBCT), the Army's current approach to a rapidly deployable, full-spectrum fighting unit, has employed Near-Term Digital Radios (NTDR)[10] that utilize a hierarchical scheme (see Figure 1.5). However, opportunities to employ and test these networks within the SBCT have been limited thus far (Toomey, 2003). The continued development and testing of such techniques and schemes (e.g., advanced antennas, advanced network architectures, smart routing schemes) is important in terms of enhancing network capacity.

---

[10] The NTDR radios employed are considered experimental. They are intended to serve as a backbone network that facilitates brigade-to-battalion communications. An NTDR network is not large; quoting *Army Communicator* (2002): "The NTDR system is a mobile packet-data radio network that links TOCs in a brigade area. Its main purpose is to provide data transport for automated systems in the Army Battle-Command System. Brigade networks of about 35 radios interoperate with other divisional networks." The primary digital communications system for the SBCT is the Enhanced Position Location Reporting System (EPLRS), which supports brigade and below units.

**Figure 1.5**
**The NTDR Hierarchical Scheme Intends to Utilize "Backbone" Nodes
to Reduce Average Path Length**

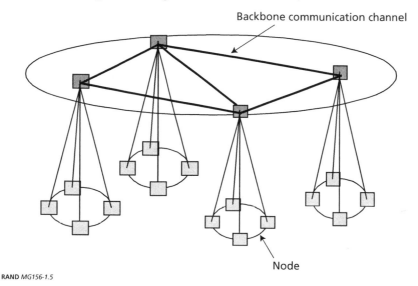

Backbone communication channel

Node

RAND *MG156-1.5*

## Problem

The Army is in the process of transforming itself from a heavy Cold War force to a much more agile one, which it has dubbed the future force. This force depends heavily on communications to enable its network-centric operations. Achieving high mobility on a rapidly changing battlefield will require considerable bandwidth, and the Army is not the only claimant—joint, coalition, and civilian organizations may be simultaneously operating in a region. Available bandwidth is affected by the required information flows that need to be supported by communications.

Networking facilitates information sharing that can tie the sensor and shooter and intermediaries into an "information grid." Because the success of the future force hinges on networked communications, the capacity of this grid (and the bandwidth, or spectral allocations, required to support such capacity) is of major concern to the Army. The G-6, U.S. Army, asked RAND Arroyo Center to determine the nature and extent of potential bandwidth problems for the future force. The key question is, Does such a grid have the capacity to handle all of the data to be transported, i.e., is its capacity sufficient to satisfy the operational requirements specified for the future force?

Figure 1.6 charts the increased demands[11] in bandwidth relative to the Gulf War in 1991. By one estimate, the Kosovo operation (Noble Anvil) doubled the amount of bandwidth used in the Gulf War (Plummer, 2003). Another estimate puts the increase at 2.5 times the Gulf War (Moseley, 2003). This substantial increase occurs

**Figure 1.6**
**Bandwidth Demand Continues to Grow**

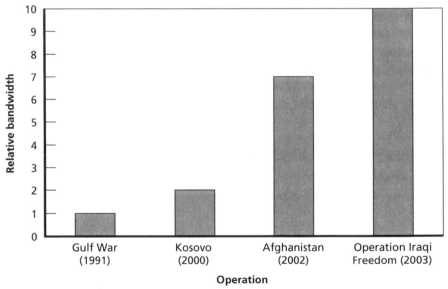

RAND *MG156-1.6*

---

[11] These estimates are aggregate snapshots of demand during the operation. As such they should be treated as indicating overall trends.

despite the fact that the force in Kosovo was only one-tenth the size of that in Desert Storm. Operation Enduring Freedom in Afghanistan represented the largest military use of bandwidth at that time and exceeded that used in the Gulf War by a factor of seven. Most recently, in Operation Iraqi Freedom (OIF), "operations require bandwidth needs roughly ten times the Gulf War according to U.S. Air Force Space Command spokesman Michael Kucharek" (Bridges, 2003). Relative growth during OIF could be even higher: "at the peak of the conflict, the Defense Information Systems Agency claimed that 3 Gbps of satellite bandwidth was being provided to the theater . . . 30 times the bandwidth made available during desert storm."

Initial assessments of future network bandwidth requirements, based on preliminary requirements documents of the future Army, highlight a gap between supply and demand. Figure 1.7 plots peak bandwidth requirements for the brigade-sized Unit of Action, as well as expectations, based primarily on spectrum available today or expected to be available in the near term. The shortfall is driven mainly by sensor data needs. This is discussed further in Chapter Three.

## Methodology

The general methodology employed for this study consisted of a combination of approaches, including literature reviews of both public and government documents, interviews with key government contractors and other Army personnel, and data analysis of the performance capabilities of certain communication technologies. Because the Army's future force concepts remain fluid, we used information and data collected during past Army digitization exercises, data on commercial devices, modeling and simulation estimates of future performance, and extensions of near-term Army plans and requirements. Specifically, we examined the operational architectures of the Stryker Brigade Combat Team and the Future Combat System to

**Figure 1.7**
**Initial Estimates Suggest Future Requirements (Demand)**
**Will Exceed Existing Supply**

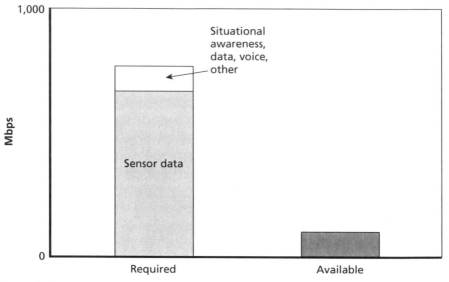

identify the key consumers of bandwidth, based on the type of information and the frequency with which it is transmitted.

This combination of approaches leads us to our assessment of where the Army is headed and what capabilities are reasonably expected to be available for the future force.

## How This Report Is Organized

The remainder of this report contains four chapters and three appendixes. Chapter Two examines the Army's current and near-term bandwidth capabilities. Chapter Three describes the concepts the Army intends to use to support its future force and what research is under way to develop them. Chapter Four outlines some ways the Army might increase bandwidth, and Chapter Five presents findings and recommendations. Appendix A describes advances in communications technology (in industry and academia) that might help the

Army address its bandwidth problem. Appendix B contains a survey of some of the routing protocols being considered for mobile ad hoc networks. Appendix C describes some of the ongoing activities addressing communications of a mobile user environment.

# CHAPTER TWO

# Current and Near-Term Capabilities

This chapter assesses the current and near-term requirement for bandwidth and the Army's capability to meet that requirement. It focuses on digitized forces, such as the Stryker Brigade Combat Team (SBCT), and on programmed system capabilities. It assesses demand in two ways: based on an analysis of information exchange, and based on data from field experiments. The discussion then turns to an analysis of how current and near-term systems support existing demands for capacity.

## Needs Based On Information Exchange Requirements

We have examined the Combined Arms Center Army Battle Command Common Operational Architecture[1] (CACACOA 3.1) to look for trends and major consumers of capacity for the SBCT. Information flows (information exchange requirements) were categorized according to their support of command, operations, administra-

---

[1] Quoting: "The CACACOA is a collection of operational architecture products that is based on the Army Universal Task List (AUTL) and the Universal Joint Task List (UJTL), that describes detailed tasks, activities, and information exchanges that occur within and among Army Units from Echelon Above Corps (EAC) to Company and below. Additionally, the CACACOA describes Army interactions with Joint and Coalition forces in the support of strategic and operational tasks. CACACOA is used to support the definition and validation of common operational requirements" (http://simci.army.mil/ds/dscgi/ds.py/ViewPropos/File-301).

tion/logistics, intelligence, fire support, and engineering. Using these categories, key consumers were identified based on the volume of information and the frequency with which it is transmitted.

- The greatest consumers appear to be database updates and transfers and sensor data. These are both voluminous and frequent. Note, however, that database and compression technologies have the potential to reduce these needs. User needs will affect the required quality of the data, which in turn affects the degree of compression used.
- The next greatest consumers are probably intelligence users, either imagery or electronic. These can be large databases but are updated only a few times per day.
- Vehicle position reports are, by far, the most frequent information passed and involve the greatest number of users. Any one report, however, is fairly small in message size.

A summary of our analysis appears in Table 2.1. These estimates are based on a best bottom-up effort to estimate demand. Although they are useful, it is important to realize that unanticipated needs can vastly increase the actual requirements. In addition, these estimates are for static or average situations that do not capture the dynamics of information flow during an operation.

**Table 2.1**
**Characterization of SBCT Information Flow from CACACOA 3.1 Data**

| Capacity Demand Versus Frequency of Communications | Less Frequent | More Frequent |
|---|---|---|
| Smaller capacity | Personnel status (6 times per day), other administrative/ logistics (1–2 per day) | Voice, combat vehicle position (240 times per day), other vehicle position (96 times per day) |
| Higher capacity | Intelligence databases from external sources, e.g., battle damage assessment (4 times per day) | Common operational picture (96 times per day), sensor data (144 times per day) |

## Needs Based on Experimental Measurements

An alternative to bottom-up estimation (from information exchange requirements) is to use actual field data, either from real operations or field experiments. Figure 2.1 shows data volumes as measured during the 1997 Division Advanced Warfighting Experiment (DAWE)[2] conducted at Fort Hood, Texas, by the 4th Infantry Division. The

**Figure 2.1**
**Brigade Communications Usage During Division**
**Advanced Warfighting Experiment**

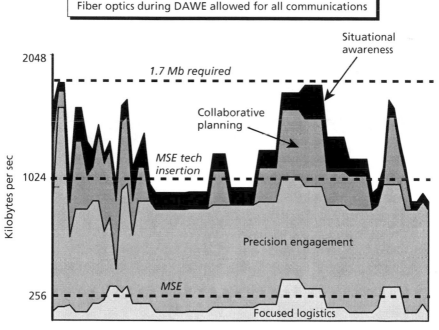

RAND MG156-2.1

---

[2] The DAWE was designed to exhibit the performance and potential for a large number of systems. For that reason, communication was basically unlimited, with nodes connected by fiber optic cable. While this is artificial, the detailed measurements do show where communications might have limited information flow.

capacity demands in this figure are at the brigade level over a 24-hour period with a breakdown according to the supported functions. The capacity demands shown in Figure 2.2 are at the division level. Specifically, the peak demand at the brigade level was 1.7 megabits per second (Mbps), and the peak communication demand at the division level is three times higher, at 5.1 Mbps.

The data from this warfighting experiment should indicate demands that change according to the phase of the battle (e.g., planning, preparation, main attack, counterattack, consolidation) and time. The data shown in Figure 2.2 are different from Figure 2.1 not only by the division level, but also by the instantaneous data that capture the dynamics of information flow over a few hours. The variation shown indicates an opportunity to "smooth demands" de-

**Figure 2.2**
**Variations in Operational Bandwidth Demands in DAWE**
**(Minus Data from Intel and Log Units)**

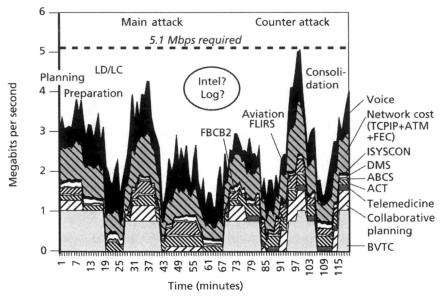

RAND MG156-2.2

SOURCE: U.S. Army Signal Center.

pending on the situation; there is a factor of five with respect to the variation from peak demand to lowest bandwidth demand. Clearly, there is an opportunity to prioritize and smooth flow throughout the network.

While in some ways reflecting dynamic needs, the DAWE was limited (as are all field experiments) by artificialities and peculiarities of the experiment as played by the forces. Command post exercises also are artificial in that play typically moves faster than it does in actual operations, and thereby increases needs for communications rates. The DAWE was designed to exhibit the performance and potential for a large number of systems. Nonetheless, these DAWE results, which show demands of 2.1 and 5.1 Mbps for the battalion- and division-level command posts, do roughly correspond to other studies of existing demand. The Congressional Budget Office (2003) cites studies by Mitre that estimate current peak demand usage to be approximately 1, 3, and 7.5 Mbps for the battalion-, brigade-, and division-level command posts respectively. A qualitative assessment[3] of the Army's AWEs (in 1997 and 1998) describes a general poor performance of the communication networks.

## Supporting Needs: Current and Near-Term Systems

Table 2.2 shows the systems that transmit the information characterized previously. The table uses the system architecture developed for the SBCT to show the number, variety, and diversity of communications networks at brigade level.

These networks are organized along functional lines, with different participants using different systems. As an example, the table

---

[3] According to the Congressional Budget Office (2003), quoting: "The Army's advanced warfighter experiments conducted at the National Training Center in 1997 and 1998 were, respectively, battalion- and brigade-level experiments using state-of-the-art communications equipment. The AWEs reveal bandwidth problems and network failures to the point where soldiers switched back to analog voice communication."

**Table 2.2**
**SBCT Information System Architecture**

| Purpose of Net | Type of Communications | Number of Users |
|---|---|---|
| Command | HF, voice | 17 |
| Situation/command and control | SINCGARS, data | 10 |
| Army Battle Command System (ABCS) Data | NTDR, data | 34 |
| Operations and intelligence | SINCGARS, voice | 31 |
| Situation/command and control | EPLRS, data | 71 |
| Command | SINCGARS, voice | 33 |
| Administration/logistics | SINCGARS, voice | 20 |
| Fire support | SINCGARS, voice | 10 |
| Total | | 226 |

NOTE: Only brigade-level networks are shown.

shows the brigade-level networks for the first SBCT. Eight networks operate at this echelon, supporting command, situation/C2, database sharing (Army Battle Command System), administration/logistics, and fire support. The networks use a variety of radio systems: single-channel ground and airborne radio system (SINCGARS), high frequency (HF), enhanced position location reporting system (EPLRS), or Near-Term Digital Radio (NTDR). Both voice and data are shared.

Information-sharing networks have the largest number of participants, with EPLRS having the largest at over 70 participants. This network primarily shares position reports. The EPLRS network at brigade links to other EPLRS networks at battalion. By contrast, command networks have fewer participants, reflecting use and importance.

Table 2.3 shows the capabilities of selected current and near-term Army communications systems that would support brigade echelons. Currently, the NTDR replaces the Mobile Subscriber Equipment (MSE). NTDR, in turn, is being replaced by the Tactical High Speed Data Network (THSDN), which can pass 256 kbps currently and has the potential to grow to 2 Mbps. Both systems require stationary transmission nodes during operation.

**Table 2.3**
**Assessment of Current and Near-Term System Capabilities**

|  | System | Mobility | Max Throughput |
|---|---|---|---|
| Current/ near term | Near-Term Digital Radio | Stationary nodes | 288 kbps (shared) |
|  | Tactical High Speed Data Network | Stationary nodes | 256 kbps growing to 2 Mbps |
| Far term (2007+) | WIN-T (new ORD) | Mobile | 256 kbps Blk 1 4 Mbps objective |
|  | JTRS (possible redirection by DoD) | Mobile | 2 Mbps Cluster 1 10 Mbps objective |

NOTE: WIN-T will also pick up communications currently supported by single-purpose systems such as Trojan Spirit, adding 1.2 Mbps to the loading shown on Figure 2.1.

In the far term, the WIN-T and Joint Tactical Radio System (JTRS) will add both increased capacity and greater mobility. The WIN-T Operational Requirements Document (ORD) is expected to align with future force concepts of operations. DoD now proposes JTRS as a platform to replace all current tactical data links on the battlefield.[4] The spectral efficiency (i.e., the ratio of the transmission capacity to the allocated bandwidth) of JTRS, as shown in Figure 2.3, is an improvement over existing radios and is at a level that is compatible with the latest commercial offerings. There exist advanced R&D efforts (see the subsection "BLAST" in Appendix A) that hold promise of increasing spectral efficiency tenfold.

Finally, the note to Table 2.3 makes the point that data currently passed by Trojan Spirit, an intelligence communications system, will be carried by WIN-T. This is an example of how the implementation of WIN-T will support multiple users, thus reducing

---

[4] The Assistant Secretary of Defense, Networks and Information Integration (ASD [NII]) (formerly the Assistant Secretary of Defense, Command, Control, Communications and Intelligence (ASD [C3I])), issued a June 17, 2003 memorandum amending the DoD Radio Acquisition Policy Memorandum of August 28, 1998, to require that all communications systems, including those operating above 2 GHz, be developed in compliance with JTRS/SCA.

**Figure 2.3**
**Spectral Efficiency of Various Radios**

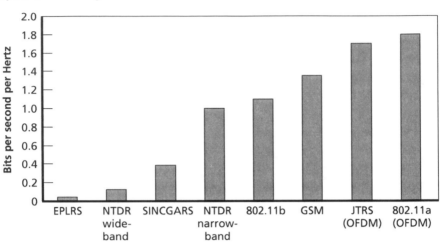

redundancy in communications. It also indicates how the demand for WIN-T will continue to increase.

## Summary and Conclusions

This chapter examined near-term demand and capabilities. Current radios and networks (NTDR and THSDN) are far less capable than the newer radios and systems being developed (JTRS and WIN-T). The newer systems will support higher data rate transmissions and communication on the move.

Measurements from the DAWE indicate that demands for capacity can easily reach and exceed 2–5 Mbps for the current digitized force, which would strain existing radio networks (NTDR and EPLRS) depending on how the network traffic is allocated. These measurements are taken in an exercise environment and hence represent demands for only a narrow slice of a real operation. However, it is apparent that current and near-term systems will not meet capacity or mobility needs of the current force. Far-term (2007+) systems will meet the needs of the current force, but demands can also be expected to grow in the interim. A Defense Science Board report (Howard, 2000) cited several sources[5] when it estimated demand in 2010 to be ten times today's levels. (The data does show an opportunity to manage operational demands and thereby reduce peak needs.)

More experimentation is needed to understand the true needs and capabilities of current and interim systems in terms of the necessity of information requirements and the manner in which various types of information contribute to mission success. At some levels, this is a sentiment shared within the Army signal community: "The Army has only fielded its first two SBCTs, and there are not enough planned training events to test the full employment of the command, control, communications, computers, intelligence, surveillance, and reconnaissance (C4ISR) and completely evaluate the commanders' ability to gain information superiority" (Toomey, 2003). Currently, there exists only a scant amount of data on the details of real-world demands and analysis of the necessity and value of proposed information flows at each of the various echelons.

With respect to analyzing information exchange requirements versus analyzing data from experimentation, both approaches provide useful insights, but neither is definitive. In general, estimates of future bandwidth should consider both procedures and allow for considerable variation and flexibility.

---

[5] The C4ISR Mission Assessment Study from 1994, the JASON Global Grid Study from 1992, and the Tactical Battlefield Communications Study from 1999.

# CHAPTER THREE

# Future Communication Needs and System Capabilities

---

This chapter examines future bandwidth needs and capabilities. It begins with a description of the Future Combat Systems concept, which is to be supported with an information grid composed of a layered communication network (see Figure 3.1). Included in these layers are (1) the terrestrial network that supports mounted troops, (2) a terrestrial network that supports dismounted troops, (3) an airborne network of unmanned aerial vehicles (UAVs) and fixed-wing aircraft at various altitudes, and (4) a space-based network of satellites. The chapter discusses communication challenges and opportunities at each of these network layers. This will be followed by a brief discussion on the issues associated with interconnecting these layers. The chapter concludes with a summary, which includes a projection of the emerging Future Combat Systems (FCS) communication concepts.

## Future Combat Systems Concept

The Army's FCS will form the building blocks for the future force. The FCS is envisioned to be a system-of-systems consisting of multifunction vehicles operating in concert. Ad hoc mobile communication networks capable of near-instantaneous transmission of data, information, and orders will connect these vehicles and their parent units. As depicted in Figure 3.1, the concept calls for a multipart information grid—a space grid, airborne grid, and terrestrial grid—to

**Figure 3.1**
**Layers of the Infosphere**

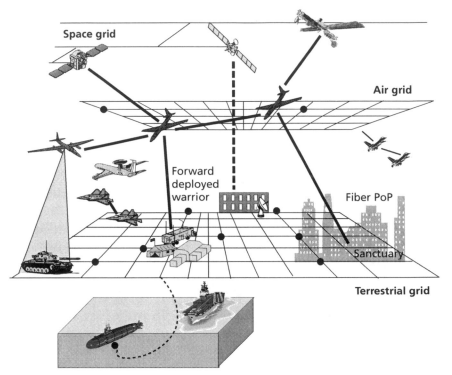

SOURCE: DARPA.

connect space-air-surface platforms to facilitate information dominance. An FCS Unit of Action is a brigade-sized force composed of
three combined arms battalions along with a "brigade" company
(HHC), an aviation detachment (AVN), a forward support battalion
(FSB), a non-line-of-sight battalion (NLOS Bn), and a C4ISR unit or
brigade intelligence company (BIC) (for network management and
other signal functions). This organization is shown in Figure 3.2. The
future force will utilize multiple Units of Action.

**Figure 3.2**
**FCS Unit of Action**

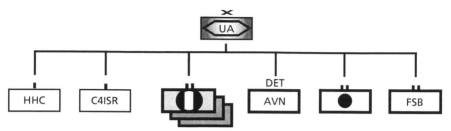

RAND *MG156-3.2*

NOTE: The symbols in the figure reflect unit size. The "x" above the UA rectangle de-
notes a brigade-sized unit. The symbol | above the HHC denotes a company-sized unit.
The text "DET" above the AVN unit reflects that the aviation unit is a detachment. The
symbol || above FSB reflects that it is a battalion-sized unit.

## Future Needs

In the introduction to this report, Figure 1.7 highlighted the preliminary estimates for bandwidth/communication-capacity and showed
the potential gap between supply and demand. It also pointed out
how sensor data dominates demand. A more detailed breakdown of
this estimate of requirements is shown in Figures 3.3 and 3.4.
Clearly, UAV sensors contribute the bulk of the requirements. Efforts
to address shortfalls certainly require curtailing these requirements.
On a unit basis, the UAV sensor data impacts the combined arms
(CA) battalions of the Unit of Action. Figure 3.3 shows the relative
breakdown of bandwidth needs. A number of data types are distin-
guished, including voice, situational awareness (SA) data, firing data,
ground robotic controls and sensors, and UAV sensors. But the relative magnitude of the UAV sensor data effectively creates two categories of data, UAV sensors and all others. Figure 3.4 shows the breakdown of demands within a Unit of Action.

**Figure 3.3**
**Unit of Action Bandwidth Requirements: Breakdown by Demand**

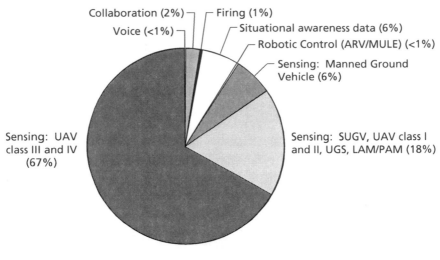

**Figure 3.4**
**Peak Requirements (Mbps) by Unit for the Unit of Action**

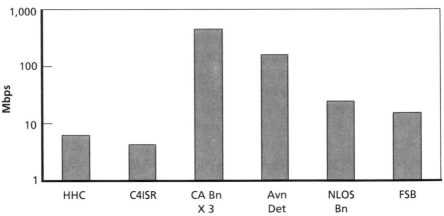

By examining the requirements documents,[1] we can extrapolate capacity demands. For the Unit of Action brigade (see Figure 3.4), the requirement suggests that peak and average capacity are on the order of hundreds of megabits per second. Based on initial studies by the Lead System Integrator (Boeing/SAIC) for the FCS, this is at least double (and perhaps 10 times) what will be available given available spectrum allocations (i.e., bandwidth). Thus, the shortfall between what is required and what is available is hundreds of megabits per second for the Unit of Action brigade.

## Challenges and Opportunities

The next several sections focus on needs and capabilities at the specific network layers (soldier, terrestrial, air, space). Overall, the performance of many of the FCS communication technologies has yet to be thoroughly tested for suitability with respect to FCS requirements. So, data are scarce. In lieu of such data, this report describes key variables that affect the performance of these technologies. For concepts where commercial technologies are relevant, those technologies will be described in terms of their performance.

## Overall Terrestrial Network

Tactical communication networks, in a network-centric environment, will certainly be mobile and "ad hoc." This is true for soldier networks and also for the larger terrestrial networks supporting ground vehicles. Ad hoc networks are, by definition, self-configuring communication networks without any central controller. A large-scale, ad hoc network of transmitting and receiving nodes is the objective for the future C4ISR architecture for FCS and the future force.

---

[1] TRADOC Pamphlet 525-3-90, *Objective Force Maneuver Units of Action*, Fort Monroe, VA: U.S. Army Training and Doctrine Command, November 1, 2002.

### Terrestrial Network Challenges

Ad hoc networks do not rely on a fixed infrastructure, such as that which a commercial cell phone network enjoys, e.g., there is no intent to use permanent towers to relay messages to and from other users/nodes. The nodes of ad hoc networks themselves have to serve this purpose, i.e., they have to store and forward each other's data packets much like today's wired Internet. The amount and type of data traffic these networks can support functionally defines their capacity.

The theoretical capacity limitations of mobile ad hoc networks (MANETs) continue to be investigated. Gupta and Kumar's (1999) results, which assume the use of omnidirectional antennas, are as follows: If we define capacity as the average rate of data transmission between any two-networked nodes (in bits per second), then the maximum capacity per node (1) decreases[2] as in $\sqrt{n}$ as $n$ gets large in a planar network, as shown in Figure 1.4, and (2) decreases as in $\sqrt[3]{n}$ for a 3-D network. While such theoretical results are useful in terms of attempting to identify limiting parameters, communication network performance can be very sensitive to scenario specific assumptions (i.e., terrain, mobility, vehicle sizes, weather, etc.).

In ad hoc networks, a message from a source node to a destination node "hops" between intermediary nodes if necessary. This is why ad hoc networks are sometimes called "multihop" networks. However, these hops consume network capacity. The bigger the network in terms of nodes $n$, the longer the chains of hops that will take place (e.g., a 9-node network may average three hops between source and destination, a 16-node network may average four hops, a 25-node network will average five hops, etc.) The rub: there is a limit to the number of capacity-consuming hops that can occur before the network traffic grinds to a halt. Thus, there is a limit to the number

---

[2] The paper by Gupta and Kumar (1999) shows capacity (of a fixed ad hoc network with nodes $n$ randomly placed) is $O(1/\sqrt{n}$ ) bits per second on a per-node basis. In other words, throughput available to each node goes to zero as the number of nodes goes up. Their work assumed omnidirectional antennas and did not account for overhead message traffic.

of nodes in such a network. But using higher-data-rate radios to improve link capacities will help.

However, it is not just the hopping of data packets that contributes to capacity utilization, but the overhead associated with routing the data. Mobile ad hoc networks must "discover" appropriate routes from sender to receiver. As an example of how this need is addressed, there are a number of commercial protocols that rely on frequent broadcasts to all network nodes to gain a picture of the network as it continues to change. But these protocols may not be appropriate in all situations (e.g., tactical environment or a congested network); protocols designed specifically for the Army may need to be developed.

## Terrestrial Opportunities: Factors Affecting Capacity in Ad Hoc Networks

A number of key parameters affect the ability to transmit information in a network of transceiving nodes. Some key factors include:

**Message routing.** Algorithms that discover routes for data packets with fewer hops and without incurring much overhead will yield relatively higher capacities. Capacity (per-node) will still diminish as the network size grows. But better routing could potentially change the shape of the curve in Figure 1.4.

**Power management schemes.** Transmission power management or "power-based routing" allows nodes to automatically either (1) increase power to get better range/connectivity, or (2) decrease power to lower the possibility of interfering with another node's transmission.

**Antenna technology.** Directional antennas can focus their energy to specific receivers, thus lowering the possibility of interference elsewhere in the network and also saving transmission energy for the node itself.

**Node mobility.** Node mobility (i.e., acceleration, speed, proximity to other nodes, etc.) affects throughput in ad hoc networks. Wilson (2001) uses GloMoSim to examine the sensitivity of message routing to vehicle mobility. He observed that throughput went down with increases in velocity when a small number of vehicles were involved. Grossglauser and Tse (2001) observed an opposite effect in their experiments that showed how mobility could improve connectivity and hence throughput. More experimentation and simulation are needed to examine how mobility impacts network performance.

**Differences between measured and theoretical performance.** The interaction of all these factors affects overall network performance. Any performance estimate is therefore a function of numerous variables whose values are neither established in a common scenario nor commonly defined. Users, thus, must carefully consider any network performance estimates as representing best-case conditions. As an example of the differences between actual and theoretical maximum data rates, Table 3.1 lists some protocols that have been used or are under development along with their theoretical and realistic data throughputs.

Estimates of realistic maximum throughput are roughly one-third to one-half the stated maximum. These estimates are documented in Dornan (2002):

> The theoretical maximum capacity of 802.11b is 11 Mbps, which is often quoted by vendors and by groups such as WECA. It pushes wireless LANs through an important psychological barrier, matching the speed of the original Ethernet standard. However, the number is misleading. It refers to the total physical layer capacity, much of which is used by the protocol itself, so it is not actually available for data. The maximum data rate of an 802.11b network is really only about 6 Mbps, and that can be achieved only under an optimum condition—over a short range and with no interference. It quickly drops when packet collisions or other errors occur. A 50% error rate will reduce the real-throughput by about two-thirds to only 2 Mbps.

Table 3.1 identifies commercial-off-the-shelf (COTS) concepts that suggest that terrestrial and soldier networks[3] seeking link

---

[3] Soldier networks are those networks that support the need for dismounted infantry to exchange voice and data. ITT Industries has demonstrated the Soldier Level Integrated Communications Environment (SLICE), a mobile computer with a headset display and micro-

throughputs around 2 Mbps are conceivable. Based on the data in the table, sensor data could easily consume this capacity. More demonstrations are needed to validate feasibility. As this section points out, there are requirements that can be relaxed on the technology side; a less mobile and/or less ad hoc network could accommodate higher data rates if demonstrations show that ground-based networks are not fully capable of higher (> 64 kbps) and reliable data rates in a tactical environment.

## Soldier Network

Soldier networks support dismounted troops. These networks pose the most challenging problem to mobile ad hoc networks, as soldiers

**Table 3.1**
**Protocols for Wireless Area Networks Are Being Developed (Commercially) with High Potential Throughputs But Realize Far Less**

| Standard | Theoretical Capacity | Realistic Data Throughput | Frequency | Multi-plexing Scheme | Status |
|---|---|---|---|---|---|
| IEEE 802.11-FH | 1 Mbps | 0.5 Mbps | 2.4 GHz | FHSS | Obsolete |
| IEEE 802.11-SS | 2 Mbps | 1 Mbps | 2.4 GHz | DSSS | Obsolete |
| IEEE 802.11b | 11 Mbps | 6 Mbps | 2.4 GHz | DSSS | Popular |
| IEEE 802.11g | 54 Mbps | 31 Mbps | 2.4 GHz | OFDM | Near future |
| IEEE 802.11a | 54 Mbps | 31 Mbps | 5 GHz | OFDM | New |
| ETSI HiperLAN1 | 23 Mbps | Unknown | 5 GHz | TDMA | Abandoned |
| ETSI HiperLAN2 | 54 Mbps | 31 Mbps | 5 GHz | OFDM | Near future |
| Home RF | 1 Mbps | 0.5 Mbps | 2.3 GHz | FHSS | Obsolete |
| Home RF2 | 10 Mbps | 6 Mbps | 2.4 GHz | FHSS | Endangered (market) |
| 5-WING/5-UP | 104 Mbps | 72 Mbps | 5 GHz | OFDM | Future |

FHSS: frequency hopping spread spectrum; DSSS: direct sequence spread spectrum; OFDM: orthogonal frequency division multiplexing; TDMA: time division multiple access.

phone; it is supposed to create a mesh (mobile ad hoc network) that handles voice communication and maps whereabouts of dismounted infantry (Krane, 2002).

are mostly dispersed into surrounding terrain and equipped with radios with limited capabilities. Soldier networks cannot be compared to commercial products connecting mobile users, as soldier networks will not be able to use an existing fixed infrastructure nor will they operate in the open. Soldier networks thus present a unique set of challenges and opportunities, as described in this section.

### Soldier Network Challenges

The soldier network is a subnet of the terrestrial network. The most basic communication requirements for dismounted soldiers are to know (1) their own location, (2) the location of friends, and (3) the location of enemies. Transmission power and antenna size will be limited to what can be practically worn and battery-powered. In buildings, tunnels, and similar locations, geolocation via GPS is extremely limited. Nonetheless, the subnet of dismounted troops will be required to maintain connectivity to the main terrestrial network and/or the information grid in general.

### Soldier Network Opportunities: New Programs and Systems

A Defense Advanced Research Projects Agency (DARPA) program to support soldier communication called Small Unit Operations Situation Awareness System (SUO SAS) was concluded in fall 2002 with successful demonstrations of the ability of dismounted soldiers to maintain communication connectivity in challenging environments. Radio ranging with accuracy of four meters was also demonstrated. SUO SAS program goals[4] were to develop radio systems that can provide the dismounted soldier the critical situational awareness required. CERDEC (the CECOM Research, Development, and Engineering Center) is funding continued development in this area under the Soldier Level Integrated Communications Environment (SLICE) program.

---

[4] As part of this effort, ITT was to develop a 4 Mbps software radio with ranging capabilities. This work continues under CECOM funding. SUO SAS has been demonstrated. SLICE will not be demonstrated until summer 2004.

More broadly, key objectives of the research program include development of the following: (1) radios that supported mobile ad hoc networking, and (2) software and hardware to facilitate continuous position/navigation and ranging ability, as well as tools that can smartly manage[5] the amount and type of information being displayed to individual soldiers. Connecting the soldier subnet to the info grid may require airborne relays, space-based relays, or both.

## Airborne Networks

The preceding sections discussed some of the difficulties with terrestrial communications. One solution to improve performance is to use an airborne or satellite-based element in the network. This adds connectivity to users who might be separated from other nodes (because they are out of range and/or out of sight) and also eases difficulties in routing messages through the network. Satellite nodes are discussed in a later section.

### Airborne Network Layer Challenges

An airborne layer can provide connectivity over rough terrain for situations where ground-to-ground communication is difficult (e.g., poor line of sight, etc.). Greater connectivity in a network can produce additional capacity-carrying links. In this manner, the UAV as a "vertical node" is a capacity multiplier. One of the key challenges with respect to relying on UAVs as vertical nodes is the number required to provide a given force size with assured connectivity. There is also the potential that such an airborne node can unintentionally limit message traffic, e.g., "exposed terminal problem" (see Karn, 1990).

---

[5] The intent of the developers was to embed an information management system that "uses knowledge of soldiers' locations and missions to automatically route the right information to the right user at the right time" (SRI, 2001).

### Airborne Network Opportunities: Adding a Vertical Node

Vertical nodes can reduce message routing duties and message routing overhead for tactical networks. Specifically, vertical nodes can be positioned to acquire routing information with fewer disruptive blanket interrogations (i.e., broadcasts) of the entire neighborhood of network nodes.

Social network analysis says that a very small number of mobile "agents" among a group can improve the information-exchange ability of the entire group.[6] This is called the "small-world" concept or "small-world" phenomenon. Work by Helmy (2002, 2003) extended this social network result to communication networks and MANETs as well as fixed sensor networks. His analysis consisted of simulation experiments of 1,000 nodes over a square kilometer. His observation of the effect of the creation of a small number of additional network paths was that it reduced the average path length for network messages (e.g., number of hops reduced). Quoting Helmy from Patch (2002): "In a network of 1,000 nodes and around 5,000 links, adding 25 to 150 links achieves 40 to 60 percent reduction in path length." We apply this observation later in this report to analyze throughput improvements for a given number of vertical nodes.

Essentially, the use of "contacts" (or short-cut-providing nodes) amounts to another layer on top of a flat network, hence a multilayer network structure with vertical nodes. The small-world contact node is essentially a MANET backbone node or a vertical node. (The choice of the node to serve in this role is based on its coverage and could be dynamically picked or designated in advance.) It is easy to envision a fleet of airborne relay nodes serving as dedicated shortcuts,

---

[6] Quoting a survey by Sanchez and Chowell-Puente (2001): "Watts and Strogatz knew that regular networks have longer path lengths and larger clustering coefficients (a measure of the fraction of a node's links that go to other nodes in its immediate vicinity) than random networks. However, they noticed that the replacement (with low probability) of a few local connections with long-term connections drastically decreases the average-path length while keeping high levels of clustering . . . Watts and Strogatz showed that the replacement of one percent of the connections of a regular network with distant links was enough to trigger small-world phenomena."

i.e., an upper layer as shown in Figure 1.5. More study is needed to determine the ideal ratio of vertical (or contact nodes) to the other network nodes.

## Space Networks

Airborne platforms are subject to weather, and they require some deployed infrastructure to support operations. Satellites are globally available, are in place for support, and add the advantages to a terrestrial network of an airborne node. They pose a different set of opportunities and challenges, as discussed in this section.

### Space Network Challenges: Limitations of Optical Links

The Transformational Communication Architecture (TCA) proposes a space grid that uses laser communications to meet future capacity requirements. As Figure 3.5 shows, absolute capacity requirements now and in the future are measured in the gigabits per second.

**Figure 3.5**
**Capacity Challenges for DoD as of June 2002**

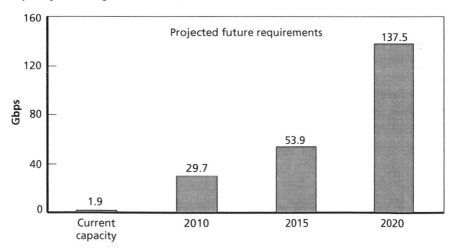

RAND MG156-3.5

SOURCE: Haven (2003).

Laser communications are feasible in space because of the predictable behavior and the relatively stable path between satellites. A key technology challenge is the link from space to ground and the optical links that exist somewhere in between. These challenges are described in this section.

Optical frequencies, perhaps in the range of $10^{13}$ to $10^{15}$ Hz, can be used for high-data-rate communication. For high data rates, optical crosslinks are better than microwave crosslinks because they can achieve very narrow bandwidths and high gains with reasonable size. Compared to the RF crosslinks, the optical systems (e.g., direct detection and heterodyne) require smaller antenna diameters.

RF crosslinks are better suited for data rates less than about 100 Mbps because of their lower mass and power. However, the development of more efficient lasers and lighter steerable optics may soon make lower rate optical links attractive.

However, optical performance degrades in the atmosphere. Table 3.2 shows how absorption varies with different atmospheric conditions.

**Table 3.2**
**Optical Link Performance Is Attenuated in the Atmosphere**

| Weather | Precipitation | Visibility | dB per km Loss at 785 nm |
|---------|---------------|------------|--------------------------|
| Dense fog | | 0–50 m | >340 |
| Thick fog | | 50–200 m | 85–340 |
| Moderate fog | | 200–500 m | 34–85 |
| Light fog | Cloudburst (100 mm per hour) | 500–1,000 m | 14–34 |
| Thin fog | Heavy rain (25 mm per hour) | 1–2 km | 7–14 |
| Haze | Medium rain (12.5 mm per hour) | 2–4 km | 3–7 |
| Light haze | Light rain (2.5 mm per hour) | 4–10 km | 1–3 |
| Clear | Drizzle (0.25 mm per hour) | 10–20 km | 0.5–1 |
| Very clear | | >20 km | <0.5 |

In clear conditions, with visibility of 20 kilometers or better, atmospheric attenuation of about 0.5 dB/km is similar to the attenuation of single-mode fiber optic cable. In haze, with visibility of 4 kilometers, the attenuation is about 3dB/km, which is similar to multimode fiber.

Visibility in clouds ranges from 15 to 150 meters, making clouds comparable to dense or thick fog. The cumulonimbus clouds in thunderstorms can be as much as 10 kilometers high. Trying to pass an optical signal through such a cloud could result in extremely high attenuation (Kim, McArthur, and Korevaar, 2001).

### Space Network Opportunities: New Technologies and Systems

**Department of Defense activities.** The TCA is being developed by NSSA (National Security Space Architect) to increase Department of Defense communications capacity. The TCA is a result of the transformation communication study that proposed an increased intersystem connectivity via optical crosslinks.

Figure 3.6 shows a notional system diagram for the TCA. The current plan is to put in place a laser communications backbone on a satellite system in geostationary orbit that would interface through radio frequency communications with warfighters worldwide.

The TCA affords the Army an opportunity to gain access to high-capacity (multiple gigabits per second) communications, certainly important for communications at theater and national echelons. Current plans for TCA will establish a global network beginning with fiber optic–based and proceeding to satellite-based optical systems. The RF link to tactical users, though, remains to be defined and funded.

**Commercial activities.** Free Space Optical (FSO) links have been used for high-bandwidth communication between buildings. Commercial systems for this purpose are typically rated by their maximum range in hazy conditions, and typical ranges are 1,000–4,000 meters. In thick fog, a 4,000-meter system is usable for up to 440 meters. In dense fog, it is usable for up to 140 meters. Clearly, systems of this class cannot communicate through thick clouds.

**Figure 3.6**
**Proposed TCA Increases Cross-link Capacity Using Optical and RF Links**

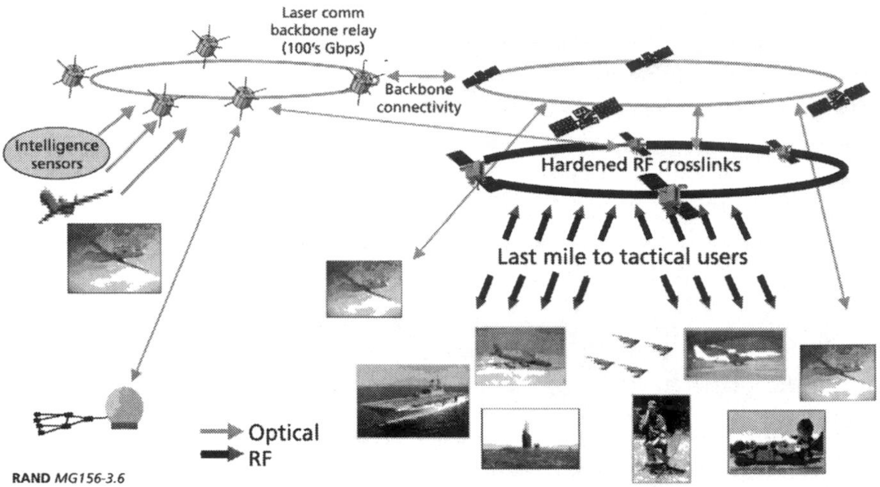

Laser comm
backbone relay
(100's Gbps)

Backbone
connectivity

Intelligence
sensors

Hardened RF crosslinks

Last mile to tactical users

→ Optical
→ RF

RAND MG156-3.6

Different wavelengths are affected differently by atmospheric conditions. Therefore, transmitting the same information in more than one wavelength increases the chance that the information will get through on at least one channel. For example, in light fog there is less scatter in the infrared than in the visible spectrum. In addition, noise levels (such as solar background noise) also vary across the spectrum.

Most applications of multispectrum optical communication are using additional wavelengths to increase capacity of the link. If, instead, the extra bandwidth is used to transmit redundant information, the extra capacity can be traded off for improved signal-to-noise ratios.

Another mechanism to address the problem of atmospheric turbulence is to transmit several beams (not necessarily on different wavelengths) that are physically displaced. Because each of these beams will experience different turbulence cells in the atmosphere, it is more likely that at least one will be experiencing quiescence at any given time.

While the ranges of these commercial systems are limited, they could be used to support selected high-capacity needs in a nonmobile scenario. These results illustrate, however, the difficulty of using optical systems near the ground in low parts of the atmosphere.

## Network Architecture: Interconnections Among the Layers

Developing an architecture for a layered communication network is a complex undertaking. Under contract to ASA(ALT), Johns Hopkins/Applied Physics Laboratory assessed alternative communication architectural topologies for the FCS, based on a bottom-up estimate of information exchange requirements. Interim reports from this study effort suggest a layered, hierarchical communication network that relies heavily on directional antennas and UAVs as communication relays. Other studies by the FCS Lead System Integrator (Boeing/SAIC) are ongoing to assess the degree of hierarchical structure needed to meet the information exchange needs of the FCS. Thus, this remains an open issue. The choice of architecture could have a significant effect on bandwidth needs and capabilities.

Specifically, Johns Hopkins University (2002) recommended a three-level hierarchical network consisting of a main network of nodes for the Unit of Action, which supports subnetworks that can interface through any of the Unit of Action nodes. Units of Action interface with each other through gateway nodes at the Unit of Employment layer, which acts as a hub. Quoting (Hillman et al, 2002): "A flat architecture at the lowest echelons exploits mobile ad hoc networking with directional antennas for terrestrial communications." According to the report, company-sized units would each need at least 2 UAV relays centrally located above them.

As an aside, the authors of the Johns Hopkins University study arrived at the following general findings: (1) unprocessed sensor data are the major data source on the network, (2) image compression techniques can reduce capacity demands, (3) the communication demand from robotic vehicles is terrain-dependent, (4) omnidirectional communications cannot achieve necessary link ranges and directional antennas will be needed, and (5) terrestrial line-of-sight communication will not be sufficient and UAVs and satcom relays will be crucial (Hillman et al., 2002).

## Summary and Conclusions

This chapter examined far-term capabilities and needs based on specification of the FCS and future force. Tiered, hierarchical architectures that use airborne and/or satellite-based systems will have to be employed. Pure terrestrial systems will probably not provide the connectivity required in dispersed operational employments. The Army envisions future systems that involve a multitiered backbone, from the ground up to space, which will compose the Global Information Grid (GIG). This implies a large degree of complexity.

Capabilities at each of the layers (terrestrial, airborne, and space) were considered by looking at the devices and networks being proposed by DARPA and others. The GIG may have to support data rates as high as hundreds of gigabits per second. At the tactical, ground level, the data rate need could be hundreds of megabits per second. Raw sensor data (from UAVs) are major contributors to these requirements. It is not clear, given existing spectral allocations, that these rates are supported by the envisioned hardware and software concepts for the near term. The required sensor usage envisioned for the future force is so large that it can be said that data needs fall into two categories: (1) those generated by sensors (very high volume) and (2) those for command and control, situational awareness, and voice traffic. Constant, iterative analysis will be required to determine data needs from among the data demands specified.

# CHAPTER FOUR

# Ways to Increase Capacity

Three general approaches to increase network capacity are as follows: (1) get the most out of the hardware and software, i.e., use improved radios and antennas and make better use of allocated spectrum; (2) get the most out of the network's architectural options, e.g., employ hierarchical schemes using vertical nodes; and (3) look for ways to keep and trim capacity demands down to what is needed.

Table 4.1 presents a categorization of ways to increase capacity along with rough estimates (some are speculative) of the relative benefits that might be achieved. It is not clear that combinations of techniques produce cumulative gains in all cases. Some techniques promise relative improvements of an order of magnitude or less. Others promise improvements of perhaps up to two orders of magnitude (e.g., directional antennas). Finally, some techniques hold the potential for several or more order-of-magnitude improvements in capacity (e.g., compression and fusion).

## Increasing Capacities of Links

Increasing the capacity of individual links can be accomplished by access to higher-frequency bands. Figure 4.1 highlights the current military use of communications spectrum. Most of the use is at the lower frequencies that are currently crowded by legacy systems. Mili-

**Table 4.1**
**Techniques to Increase Bandwidth**

| Technique | Specifics and Potential Improvements |
| --- | --- |
| Increase capacities of links | Higher frequencies and optical frequencies (×10), frequency reuse and spectral-efficient radios (×2–20), directional antennas (×2–300) |
| Improve routing efficiency | Use new protocols for ad hoc networks, i.e., smarter routing and/or node aggregation and clustering (×2–10) |
| Add a vertical element | Airborne or satellite increases connectivity/decreases network load (×2–4) |
| Adjust needs of applications | Incorporate communications into database architecture (JCDB); data compression and fusion (multiple orders-of-magnitude improvement) |
| Manage bandwidth operationally | Treat bandwidth as a limited operational resource (×3–5) |

tary uses, however, can conflict with commercial interests in spectrum; foreign and U.S. commercial interests also have made allocations in these bands scarce.

Currently, commercial mobile users are not planning to use higher frequencies. DARPA is developing FCS communications systems around 38 GHz, which provides increased inherent bandwidth and improved low probability of detection and intercept, but which complicates antenna design.

Efficient use of frequency allocations can also improve capacity. Figure 4.2 illustrates a plot of measured spectrum occupancy collected over 43 minutes using an elevated (50-foot) antenna for reception in an urban area. Note the variations in receiver power and the noticeable slices of unused spectrum. The figure shows that adaptive spectrum management can increase capacity by more efficient use of spectrum.

## Figure 4.1
## Military Can Use Higher Frequencies

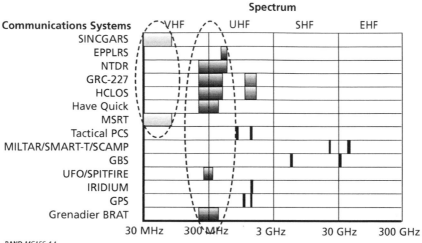

RAND *MG156-4.1*

SOURCE: CECOM. Used with permission.

## Figure 4.2
## Fixed Spectrum Assignments Lead to Inefficient Utilization

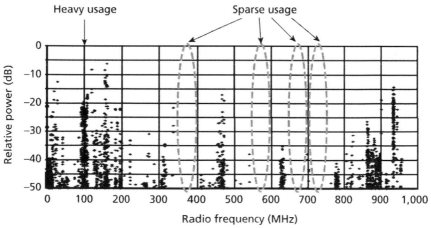

RAND *MG156-4.2*

SOURCE: Horne (2003). Used with permission.

Reuse can be accomplished with the use of existing wireless waveform applications with either automated adaptive approaches or reassignment of channels by the military commanders. The DARPA XG program aims to seek technologies that provide relative improvements on the order of 10–20 times the capabilities of conventional radios (see Appendix C).

## Utilizing Directional Antennas

Omnidirectional antennas transmit and receive in all directions. For communication between a specific sender-receiver pair, this is a waste of energy and causes unwanted interference with other transmitters and receivers that are nearby. The concept of directional antennas is that the beam of the transmission is more focused, i.e., "less energy in the wrong directions, more energy in the right directions." Directional antennas improve routing efficiency by focusing network routing along uncongested routes and by reducing redundant flows in the network.

Two categories of directional antennas are switched beam and steered beam. In a switched beam arrangement, the antenna is made up of multiple, predefined narrow beams so that individual beams can be selected. Switched beam antennas can be made cheaply and small (Ramanathan, 2003). A steered beam antenna has a single main lobe that can be redirected, i.e., an algorithm steers a main lobe and nulls (Jain, 2003). A steered beam is more complex but performs better than a switched beam.

Gupta and Kumar (1999) show that network capacity does not scale well and that, at best, per-node capacity is $O(1/\sqrt{n})$. This theoretical result does not take into account directional antennas. A recent paper by Yi, Pei, and Kalyanaraman (2003) calculates the capacity improvements from using directional antennas, relative to a network that uses omnidirectional antennas. For a random network, they prove that the relative gain from using directional antennas is $\dfrac{2\pi}{\alpha}$ if just the sender or the receiver relies upon a directional antenna of beamwidth $\alpha$. If both the senders and receivers of data utilize directional antennas, the relative improvement is $\frac{4\pi}{\alpha\beta}$, where $\alpha$ and $\beta$ are the beamwidth (in radians) of the sender and receiver respectively. Table 4.2 provides a number of example calculations. It is observed that greater gains come with narrow beamwidths. However, the more narrow the beamwidth, the more technically difficult network routing becomes, especially in a mobile environment; i.e., a narrow beam does place a greater burden on the protocol/radio to have accurate knowledge of the physical location of other radios. The DARPA FCS Communications Program has been conducting tests and demonstrations using directional antennas.

### Advantages and Disadvantages of Directional Antennas

The advantages of directional antennas are as follows:

1. Increased gain and thus longer range, which could lower the number of hops required and lower end-to-end latency;
2. Less interference and thus more spatial reuse, implying higher aggregate capacity;
3. Higher signal to noise ratio (SNR), implying better connectivity;
4. Better information assurance: narrower beamwidth, implying better security from interceptions, and better tolerance to jamming due to "nulling" capability (Ramanathan, 2003).

**Table 4.2**
**Relative Capacity Gains from Using Directional Antennas**

| Sender Beamwidth (degrees) | Receiver Beamwidth (degrees) | Relative Capacity Improvement |
|---|---|---|
| 20 | 20 | 324 |
| 30 | 30 | 144 |
| 90 | 90 | 16 |
| 20 | omni | 18 |
| 30 | omni | 12 |
| 90 | omni | 4 |

One potential disadvantage is that the longer range could inadvertently interfere with a distant radio; power control would address this issue. Also, directional antennas add cost and complexity, especially for very narrow beamwidths.

### Simulation Results Using Directional Antennas

Theoretical results are useful because they indicate how much progress can be made in terms of this technology. Simulation experiments with directional antennas tend to be more specific about type of protocol and contention scheme used. To date, simulation experiments with directional antennas show only modest improvements. Therefore, more development is required to achieve the gains that have been shown to be theoretically possible.

Ramanathan (2003) reports on OPNET simulations[1] of a network using directional antennas (steerable); relative throughput improvements were reported to be between 70 and 370 percent. Ramanathan observes that power control is important in terms of harnessing maximum performance improvements.

Sanchez (2002) reports simulation[2] results on relative throughput improvements. Table 4.3 shows ranges of how much more data are likely to get through the network with directional versus omnidirectional antennas. Sanchez varied network density: net-

---

[1] OPNET is a commercially available network simulator. Ramanthan (2003) describes the simulations as a 20-node "highly loaded" ad hoc network running UDAAN protocols (that integrate power control) and assuming steerable antennas with both transmit and receive beamforming. UDAAN (Utilizing Directional Antennas for Ad hoc Networking) is a project sponsored by DARPA under the Future Combat Systems Communications program. "A significant payoff from UDAAN will be increased effective capacity. Other payoffs include decreased packet latency, increased connectivity, greater multicast efficiency, and lower probability of detection/interference." See http://www.ir.bbn.com/projects/udaan/udaan-index.html.

[2] Experiments by M. Sanchez (2002) varied the CSMA/CA contention scheme by changing assumptions on whether the sender and receiver use directional antennas (for data or overhead messages associated with data transfer). His results showed that the most aggressive scheme in terms of utilizing directional antennas whenever possible work best. Power control was not integrated into the scheme.

**Table 4.3**
**Throughput Improvements for Two Networks**
**Using Directional Antennas**

| Antenna Beamwidth | 90 degrees | 60 degrees | 30 degrees | 10 degrees |
|---|---|---|---|---|
| Network A | 29–64% | 43–107% | 86–143% | 56–186% |
| Network B | 6–26% | 17–39% | 72–100% | 17–145% |

work A was made to be more sparse than network B. Power control was not incorporated into his scheme.

## Improving Routing Efficiency

Effective routing schemes can use the network more efficiently, reducing redundancy in routing packets and excess overhead. Some estimates of benefits from academic research on advanced schemes show improvements of factors (delay and packet delivery ratio) up to an order of magnitude when compared with existing concepts (Blazevic, Le Boudec, and Giordano, 2003). Routing protocol development is an active area of investigation within the academic and commercial sectors, and there are gains that can be achieved by continuing to develop/refine routing protocols. Appendix B provides a description of alternative schemes.

## Adding a Vertical Element

The inherent constraints on capacity for a flat network can be dealt with by making them "unflat," i.e., creating islands of flat subnetworks that are smaller and interact with another layer of nodes. The multilevel structure allows the islands to cross communicate via "backbone" nodes, which could be UAVs. An issue is how adaptive such structures can be, i.e., can they easily be formed ad hoc, or will they require static preconfiguration? Obviously, an ad hoc formation ability is desired, but more test and demonstration is needed.

A mobile airborne node is conceptually ideal as a vertical node. In a hierarchical architecture, it can lead to better routing, i.e., it can be positioned to acquire routing information with fewer (disruptive) blanket interrogations (i.e., broadcasts) of the entire neighborhood of network nodes. It is easy to envision a fleet of airborne relay nodes serving as communication relays, i.e., an upper layer. Earlier in this report we posed the question of what is the ideal ratio of these contact nodes to regular nodes. This issue is addressed in this section.

We rely on Helmy's (2002, 2003) estimate of the number of vertical nodes required to reduce average path length in a network. We consider that an airborne node that facilitates a decrease in "average path length reduction" implies a proportional increase in network capacity (via a reduction in overhead messages and message hopping).

The result of a formulation of the number of UAVs needed to attain a certain throughput increase is shown in Figure 4.3. Depending on the terrain and network size, UAVs could increase capacity by as much as 3–4 times. (An airborne node in an urban environment will facilitate fewer shortcuts than an airborne node in a desert environment on a clear day.) While substantial improvements are possible, complex or harsh terrain could require large numbers of UAVs. The analysis shown assumes a network of 1,000 nodes as well as Helmy's experimental observation that the addition of a few link paths decreases path lengths (i.e., number of hops) by 25 percent, 150 additional links decrease path lengths by 60 percent, and 200 additional links decrease path lengths by 70 percent, etc.

UAVs are dual purpose. They can serve as vertical nodes (i.e., communications relays). They are also sensors that could conceivably create large amounts of data that contribute to congestion if passed into a network. (Command and control messaging to and from a UAV is a very small amount of message traffic in comparison.) A vexing issue is that the placement and location of the UAV dictates its most useful role. For example, a UAV placed within the borders of a brigade-sized force is useful as a communications relay for message traffic within the brigade. This may not be ideal positioning if the UAV's role is to serve as a reconnaissance asset.

**Figure 4.3**
**UAVs Add Connectivity and Capacity But Could Require**
**Large Numbers of Vehicles**

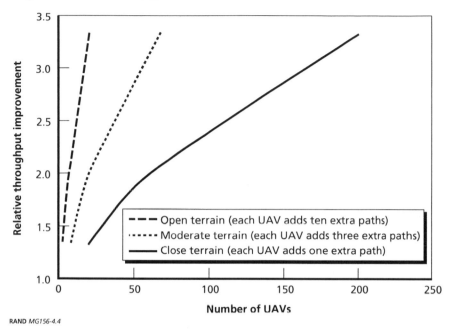

RAND *MG156-4.4*

## Adjusting Needs of Applications

Adjusting applications has great potential for reducing user demands
for bandwidth while maintaining quality. As an example, compression of voice is considered. (Although voice data will be relatively
small compared to sensor data, this is useful for highlighting the potential gains through compression; still, voice compression will be
important for certain subnets like soldier networks [e.g., SLICE].)
Figure 4.4 shows the effect of voice compression coding on bandwidth. Uncompressed digitized voice typically requires 64 kbps in a
public switched telephone network (PSTN). Bandwidth needs can
already be reduced to 2.4 kbps with acceptable voice quality. Voice
quality is maintained by sophisticated processing, taking advantage of
predictability in voice signals. Better compression trades off with

**Figure 4.4**
**Compression Reduces Bandwidth Demands, Increases Computing Demands**

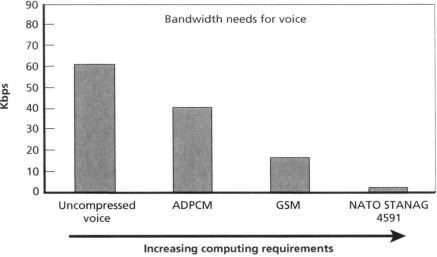

RAND MG156-4.5

computing power, e.g., more computer power required to implement better compression schemes. In general, as computing power grows faster than communications capacity, the tradeoff favors compression. Compression schemes must be evaluated, however, for quality. NATO has extensively tested voice coders. Details of the testing are described in a NATO C3 Agency report.[3]

## Managing Bandwidth

Managing operational demands can have a great impact on overall communications network performance. Opportunities to manage bandwidth depend on the time-varying nature of communications in an operational setting. Table 2.1 showed estimates for the type and

[3] NATO C3 Agency, CIS Division, "The NATO Post-2000 Narrow Band Voice Coder: Test and Selection of STANAG 4591," Technical Presentation-001.

frequency of information flow for a Stryker Brigade Combat Team. Based on projected information exchange requirements, the table showed that there is a large volume of very frequent status reporting that could be managed to meet the needs of the most stressed units in a fast-paced operation while relaxing requirements for units that are not moving or changing status.

Operational demands will also change according to the phase of the battle. Data from the Division Advanced Warfighting Experiment conducted at Fort Hood by the 4th Infantry Division (shown in Figure 2.2) illustrated how demand varies depending on the phase of the battle (planning, preparation, main attack, counterattack, consolidation). This variation indicates an opportunity to "smooth demands" depending on the situation, with variations from peak to lowest bandwidth demanded differing by a factor of three to five.

## Assessing and Comparing Improvement Techniques

Key technologies/techniques are rank ordered in Table 4.4. This table highlights the techniques that promise the greatest improvements. Communications performance, though, is not easily characterized or estimated because, for example, connectivity of any given network will vary over time and operating conditions.

The table describes some of the improvement techniques described in this report within the context of three different types of networks (e.g., a highly connected network, a moderately connected network, and a sparsely connected network). For a highly (or fully) connected network, in which users are densely packed, the table shows that vertical node usage, in an already highly connected network, is not useful and perhaps adds to congestion unnecessarily.

For the moderately connected network, in which users have some connectivity, the table points out that routing can make a large contribution to increase capacity. For a highly connected network, improved routing does not help (as all nodes are connected), and a vertical node is not needed. A vertical node could be a hindrance.

**Table 4.4**
**Relative Value of Bandwidth Techniques Depends on**
**Operational Situation (Network Topology)**

| Improvement Technique | Highly Connected Network | Moderately Connected Network | Sparsely Connected Network |
|---|:---:|:---:|:---:|
| Increase capacities of links | + | + | + |
| Improve routing | o | + | o |
| Add a vertical node | – | o | + |
| Adjust applications | + | + | + |
| Manage bandwidth operationally | + | + | + |

Note: + denotes positive improvement, o none or little, – negative. Highly connected network has all nodes directly connected to others; sparsely connected network has all nodes connected to at most two other nodes; moderately connected network has some fully connected, other sparsely connected nodes.

The last column of the table shows a sparsely connected network, representing a very dispersed force. In this case, improved routing may not improve performance, as there is only one route through the network. But the vertical node is very useful in this network to increase connectivity and reduce congestion. The point of the table is to show how different operational deployments can result in different technology rankings. Improved routing schemes and the use of vertical nodes (UAVs, SATCOM) is beneficial in some scenarios but not all. It is important to note that some of the observations discussed above are affected by terrain and network traffic, mobility, and interoperability requirements. Table 4.5 considers some of these additional factors.

Observations from Table 4.5 are as follows: Some of the technologies and concepts that increase link capacity (e.g., higher frequencies and directional antennas) complicate mobility by requiring geographical knowledge of the network topology and possible prediction of future locations. This is not an infeasible requirement, but it complicates solutions. Secure communication is helped by directional antennas but possibly complicated by improved routing and vertical node usage. Many improved routing protocols rely on de-

**Table 4.5**
**Bandwidth Improvements Trade Off with Other Performance Factors**

| Technique | Data Volume | Mobility | Secure Communication | Inter-operability |
|---|---|---|---|---|
| Increase capacity of links | + | − | + | − |
| Improve routing | + | + | − | − |
| Add a vertical node | + | + | − | + |
| Adjust applications | + | O | + | − |
| Manage bandwidth operationally | + | + | + | O |

tailed network knowledge, which, if compromised, would reveal unit locations. The vertical node increases connectivity but can also be intercepted by an enemy. Interoperability and backward compatibility are complicating requirements. They require that legacy systems be explicitly incorporated into the network design.

## Summary and Conclusions

This chapter outlined a number of means to address the need for more networking capacity. Many technologies and concepts are under development that will increase capacity of individual links. Among the technologies and concepts are the use of higher frequencies[4] and directional antennas. There is more available bandwidth at higher frequencies. Moving from 2.4 GHz to 38 GHz will increase available bandwidth and hence capacity by a factor of ten. The DARPA FCS Communications Program is experimenting with higher frequencies in this range. For the terrestrial and air grids, directional antennas (using 20–120 degree sectors) can be used; they have been shown to increase capacity by factors of up to two to four in simulation; theoretical results indicate the possibility of much more substantial improvements using this technology. In addition,

---

[4] A benefit of higher frequencies is that they can use smaller antennas.

airborne assets like UAVs and space-based satellites can provide improvements in connectivity necessary to increase capacity.

Reductions on the demand side may prove more beneficial. Reducing demand effectively increases capacity. Compression and data fusion can reduce demands by transmitting the data that has to be sent in the most efficient manner possible. Another consideration: adjust the needs of applications. For instance, database caching can reduce the distance that database updates need to travel to a user. Finally, network capacity will need to be managed operationally, i.e., treating bandwidth as a scarce resource to be allocated according to the commander's guidance and priorities. This could result in reduced and smoothed demands. All of these concepts will help close the gap between capacity demanded and capacity supplied.

Overall, it is not clear how much of the gap can be closed: The gap can be eliminated if requirements (e.g., numbers of UAV and other sensors, size and frequency of COP[5] updates, scope of information dissemination, etc.) are arbitrarily relaxed. However, requirements (demand) cannot be reduced below a level that facilitates information dominance.[6] What this level turns out to be is unclear. More experimentation and simulation can shed light on true capacity needs (versus existing requirements and demands). Based on available spectrum and projected capabilities of the technology options (radios, software protocols, antennas), it does not appear that technology alone can completely close the gap.

---

[5] COP, or common operating picture, is a key enabler for battle command. "The COP is a single fused picture containing real to near real-time information depending on echelon." Its purpose is "to enable situational understanding, decision-making and problem solving by commanders." TRADOC Pamphlet 525-3-0.1, *The Future Force C4ISR Concept (Draft)*, Fort Monroe, VA: U.S. Army Training and Doctrine Command.

[6] A condition that results from the use of offensive and defensive information operations to build a comprehensive knowledge advantage at a time, place, and on decision issues critical to mission success.

# CHAPTER FIVE

# Major Findings and Recommendations

## Major Findings

The major findings of this report are as follows. First, the capacity of communications systems planned to support the new force structure will continue to fall short of the required demand. This is based on specified requirements and proposed technologies and architectures for the future force. Furthermore, the current gap between the supply and demand of capacity will remain until either demand for capacity is reduced, or technology (satellites, UAVs, directional antennas, more radios) increases the supply, or both.

Second, a number of technologies and concepts under development show promise of increasing network capacity. Some of the communications technologies we have examined promise capacity improvements by factors of up to ten. Directional antennas have the potential to increase capacity even more if they are developed to their full potential.

Third, bandwidth will always be a limited resource, especially as user demands grow in unanticipated ways. Technology is not likely to solve this problem, especially at the wireless tactical level, so bandwidth management will be required.

Fourth, other related issues like interoperability, information assurance, and mobility (comms-on-the-move) require equal attention, i.e., more than bandwidth needs to be considered in network design and operations. Better techniques to balance tradeoffs among these sometimes competing measures are needed.

Finally, bandwidth issues are attracting considerable DoD attention, especially at theater echelons and above. The Army should take advantage of this interest and pursue additional support for the technologies and concepts that can help the Army meet its needs while focusing its own resources.

It is worth noting the commercial world's difficulty[1] in delivering high-data wireless mobile communication with infrastructure-based concepts, e.g., third- and fourth-generation phones. It will be no easier for the Army as it develops infrastructureless mobile communication with even less proven concepts, e.g., peer-to-peer MANETs. There is a also a likelihood that the Army will have to develop its own protocols to meet its unique needs, as opposed to fully leveraging commercial offerings.

## Specific Recommendations

A gap exists between the expected available capacity and the required capacity for the future force. As a result, this report describes a number of specific steps that can be taken to address the gap. In order of priority, they are as follows.

### Reassess Information Demands and Needs

The Army must perform experiments to understand what drives "real-world" information demands. There is only a scant amount of data on the details of real-world demands and analysis of the necessity and value of proposed information flows at each of the various echelons. Little testing has been carried out for large operational nets. What testing has been done has found shortfalls in bandwidth supplies. The Army must reassess the necessity of these information requests. One measure of the need for the information demanded is the manner in which said information contributes to mission success.

---

[1] Elisa Batista, "Losses Dog 3G Pioneer NTT Docomo," *Wired News*, November 1, 2002, accessed at www.wired.com/news/wireless.

## Change Application Structure

Applications determine the volume and timing of a large part of information flow. Applications improvements, in terms of compression and data fusion, have potential for order-of-magnitude reductions in bandwidth demands. Minimizing the need to transmit raw sensor data will be beneficial, especially if local fusion is feasible. However, explicit performance assessments must be conducted to maintain quality with respect to data fusion and compression.

## Manage Operational Demands to Meet Needs

Information traffic patterns exhibit differing needs for different-priority users. Changing information needs requires a dynamic network management approach to prioritize and smooth flow through the network. This has already been explicitly recommended in an Operation Iraqi Freedom after action report.[2]

## Increase Efficiency of Network Routing

Army communications are increasingly network based, and capacity issues must be addressed from a network perspective. The U.S. Army Communications-Electronics Command (CECOM), the Defense Advanced Research Projects Agency (DARPA), and commercial industry are attempting to increase network capacity via more efficient routing through networks. These techniques take advantage of knowledge of the network state to improve routing efficiency.

## Increase Capacities of Links

Both CECOM and DARPA (e.g., the FCS Communications and Next Generation Communications programs) are working to increase link capacities by using higher frequencies and directional antennas. Theoretical assessments by Yi, Pei, and Kalyanaraman (2003) show that the capacity-multiplying effect of directional antennas over to-

---

[2] Shaaber, Hedberg, and Wesson (2003) call for "The ability to manage bandwidth usage dynamically at the discretion of the commander [to allocate bandwidth] commensurate with operational priorities."

day's nondirectional (omnidirectional) antennas could be as high as one to two orders of magnitude, depending on the technology used. These are better results than what has been seen in simulation of various types of directional systems. Clearly, the opportunity for improvement exists, and more development is needed to fully realize the benefits of this concept. If directional antenna systems can be developed to their full potential, they could help ameliorate the inherent capacity limitations of large numbers of radios sharing a frequency channel.

Today's fixed, limited frequency allocation of available spectrum creates a hard limit on the amount of capacity, especially for ground vehicles on the move. Commercial demands in the United States, Europe, and other countries are squeezing the available spectrum for use by the U.S. military and its allies.[3] By one estimate, there may be as little as 55 MHz available[4] today for the Army; this could translate into 50 to 100 Mbps capacity for a given area of operation, at best. (Such limited spectrum access in CONUS also prohibits the "train as you fight" notion.) The lower end of this range may not be sufficient to accommodate one brigade-sized unit's situational awareness needs.[5]

Spectral reuse is key to achieving as much capacity as possible. Directional antennas facilitate reuse even with fixed frequency/spectral allocations. Fully dynamic spectrum management could facilitate even greater reuse of the spectrum by obviating the need for static channel/frequency assignments. DARPA is developing technologies to enable dynamic access to radio frequency spectrum.

---

[3] Quoting: "high-tech companies are lobbying to block the recent DOD proposal [to open up the 5,150 to 5,720] megahertz band to accommodate the burgeoning industry." *Inside the Pentagon*, "DoD Battles Industry on Spectrum Wanted for Wireless Networking," December 2002.

[4] This is when given only the JTRS threshold operating frequencies, which are between 2 Mhz and 2 Ghz, when considering availability for the Future Combat Systems (FCS) communication network. U.S. Army, "FCS WNW Spectrum Requirement" white paper, December 6, 2002.

[5] Assuming an average situational awareness (SA) data rate of 64 kilobits per second per vehicle/node and a 1,000+ node brigade.

This is an important technology concept that needs to continue to be developed.

## Overall Assessment and Recommendations

Bandwidth is a limited resource that needs to be managed. New technologies will greatly increase network capacity, but growing user demands will probably keep pace and exceed available capacities. No single technique will solve the problem. The Army should continue to pursue all technologies that promise benefits. However, the development of these technologies and concepts needs to be synchronized through a single cognizant agency. This includes not only communications systems but also systems-of-systems to reduce demands and create an overall information architecture.

The challenge is to meet the right users' needs at the right time. To achieve this, it is recommended that the Army treat bandwidth as an operational resource that needs to be allocated by commanders and staffs. The Army should develop and refine assessment tools; better assessment tools are needed to make complex tradeoffs. Lastly, the Army needs to make a partner of DoD to avoid unnecessary redirection and to take advantage of DoD-wide capabilities. This is especially important with respect to the DoD efforts to maintain and perhaps acquire new spectral allocations.

# Commercial Communication Technological Advances

This appendix (1) discusses the differences between commercial and Army communications concepts; (2) provides the reader an overview and description of the existing relevant commercial wireless technologies available today; and (3) discusses and explains wireless communication technologies projected to be available in the near future. While there is an overall difference in network design between the Army and commercial industry, the Army could take advantage of some of these individual technologies to address communication and bandwidth issues at the brigade and below level.

## Differences Between Commercial and Army Communications Concepts

The Army wants to leverage commercial technologies and concepts. Yet existing commercial technologies are insufficient (e.g., not set up for a mobile infrastructure) for the transformed Army, i.e., the future force. Table A.1 summarizes some of the design tradeoffs made by commercial industry and the Army in meeting user needs.

### Mobility Differences

Both military and commercial users desire to move a high volume of multimedia data among distributed users. But the two users approach mobility in a much different manner. Commercial users rely on user

**Table A.1**
**Army's Networking Needs Do Not Align with Today's Industry Focus**

| Attribute | Industry Approach | Army Approach |
|---|---|---|
| Volume and type of data | High volume, multimedia | High volume, multimedia |
| Mobility | Mobile users, fixed or predictable infrastructure | Mobile users, reconfigurable network and deployable infrastructure |
| Wireless information assurance approach | Commercial encryption | Type 1 encryption; low probability intercept/ detection; resistance to jamming |
| Interoperability | Users adjust to new standards, consensus standards | Maintain backward compatibility |
| Access to spectrum | Increase to wireless spectrum | Protect access to wireless spectrum; go to higher frequencies |
| Network architecture | Client-server | Peer-to-peer |

mobility, but connected after initial entry to either a fixed or predictable (e.g., satellite based) infrastructure for routing. The Army supports mobile users, but also must rely on a mobile and deployable infrastructure. Army communications networks must also rapidly reconfigure as the physical and operational environments change. Table A.1 highlights the differences between an industry approach and an Army approach for various attributes of a communication network.

**Wireless Information Assurance Differences**

In this report, the term "wireless information assurance" refers to protection of wireless communications. Information assurance is a broader concept, involving protection of databases, processors, and information. For our purposes, we focus only on the wireless portion. In this case, industry relies on encryption. The Army relies on encryption but also low probability of intercept/detection and on resistance to jamming.

### Interoperability Requirements Differences

Industry ultimately relies on the user for interoperability. The Army must maintain interoperability with large numbers of legacy systems, which can limit the ability to take advantage of the latest technologies. The quantity of radios in the Army might force it to operate networks with heterogeneous types of equipment.

### Spectral Access Differences

Spectrum access is an area of direct competition between industry and the Army. Most competition is currently at the 1.755–1.850 GHz frequency band, and the Army plans to maintain this and add higher frequencies in the future.

### Network Architecture Differences

Figure A.1 (taken from Grobmeier, 2002) emphasizes the quantifiable differences. In the figure, the cellular technology offered by existing commercial devices is viewed as relying far too much on fixed

**Figure A.1**
**Today's Commercial Industry Relies Heavily on Fixed Infrastructure**

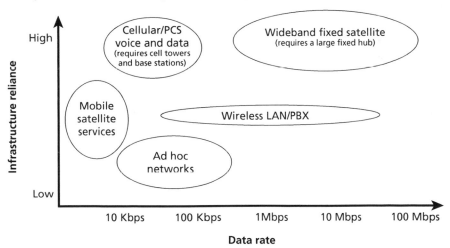

RAND MG156-A.1

SOURCE: Grobmeier (2002).

infrastructure (relative to the ad hoc networks required for the future force). The much-ballyhooed third-generation mobile phones have not been shown to be capable of the 1 Mbps data rates that were anticipated. Mobile ad hoc networks for the military may require data rate capabilities at or in excess of 1 Mbps. Despite what is shown in the chart, mobile satellite services can be considered high in terms of infrastructure reliance because they require huge investments in the space segment. Also, ad hoc networks may span across a data rate range as wide as that of the wireless LANs.

Today's commercial wireless world requires fixed infrastructure, e.g., cellular towers, base stations, etc. Thus, projections of existing commercial wireless capabilities onto future military communication capabilities are not entirely useful. However, some relevant research and development directions are being pursued in the commercial world. If these directions prove viable, these technologies and concepts will be suitable for military (e.g., mobile and ad hoc). In summary, assumptions that military communications networks can now be acquired to meet the Army's needs via commercial-off-the-shelf (COTS) technologies are unreasonable; however, future technologies under development now may bear fruit for the military. Some relevant technologies are discussed next.

## Commercial Mobile Phone Technology

The capacity of commercial radios, cell phones, and the like provide a baseline for future military capabilities. As described earlier, the transmission capacity of a single radio does not mean that the network traffic in a wireless, ad hoc network will enjoy the same high rate when multiple users/nodes are involved. Nonetheless, it's important to understand the transmission capabilities of individual radios (phones). It should be noted that the Joint Tactical Radio System (JTRS) is specified to transmit at a maximum rate of 2 Mbps.

Analog mobile phones represent the first generation (1G) of technology. These "radios" do not transmit digital data. Second-generation (2G) mobile phones are already commercially available;

there are a number of technology alternatives among the commercial offerings (e.g., Code Division Multiple Access [CDMA[1]], Global Systems for Mobile Communication [GSM[2]], and Personal Digital Cellular [PDC[3]]). Second-generation phones do digitize voice into data packets but operate at low data rates, e.g., around 10 kbps. "2.5G technology" is the term coined for commercial entrants that are upgrades of 2G mobile phones. Developers hope to achieve data rates up to 100 kbps, but these technologies are likely to achieve only half that rate at best.

The "third-generation" (3G) mobile phone technology (and personal digital assistant technology) is supposed to be able to support web access, interactive video, and CD-quality voice via data rates of at least 144 kbps. Ideal capacity for 3G is twice this minimum, with the hope of 2 Mbps as an achievable capacity under certain conditions (e.g., stationary nodes). The actual performance of initial 3G entrants into the commercial market is reportedly not much better than 64 kbps. Recently, the Japanese cellular network operator NTT DoCoMo began commercial operation of the world's first 3G system. The most advanced concepts being discussed today (called 4G technology) anticipate data rates of 100 Mbps, although predictions of such high data rates for 4G are wildly optimistic for any time frame except the far future.

---

[1] CDMA is a standard for digital communication that involves spread spectrum technology, unlike GSM and PDC. It was introduced by Qualcomm.

[2] GSM is an open, evolving standard for digital communication (supports voice, text, and data transfers) for mobile phone technology. It relies upon a version of Time Division Multiple Access (TDMA) to allow multiple users to contend for use. It is in an open standard used widely in Europe (Dornan, 2002). In the United States, T-mobile, Cingular, and AT&T operate a GSM network in the 1.9 GHz band (www.linuxsecurity.com).

[3] PDC is the second most popular cell phone standard but is mainly used in Japan. It uses a variant of TDMA but is not compatible with GSM. NTT's DoCoMo uses PDC. It operates in the 0.8 and 1.5 GHz bands.

## Wi-Fi

The popular commercial protocol for wireless communication is known as "Wi-Fi." Loosely speaking, it is a wireless version of Ethernet. It is also known by its IEEE standard number 802.11b. It is commercially available now, and the required hardware can be inexpensively acquired through a number of commercial vendors. In the long term, wireless networking could be a competing concept to 3G (or 4G) personal communication devices.

Currently, 802.11 is mostly used for low-power (less than 1 watt) wireless office networks and other local area networks. It requires a very simple-to-install card that enables wireless communications for ordinary computers. Typically, these cards are used to enable communication in what is called "infrastructure mode" so that an access point (AP) acts as a transmitting base (or server) that is usually connected to a wired network but can transmit and receive wirelessly. Appropriately equipped laptops or desktop PCs (clients) communicate with the base via RF frequency (the Industrial, Scientific, and Medical [ISM] Band[4] around 2.4 GHz), thus facilitating access to the wired network via the base that is physically connected.

In this mode, the clients must be within transmission range of the server. But 802.11b can also be implemented in what is called "infrastructureless mode," in which each client (or node) need only be in communication range of another node because each node can forward the messages of its peers. If a mobile ad hoc networking protocol were used with this hardware, then it would be a usable type of system for mobile Army units.

### Spread Spectrum

As its name implies, spread spectrum spreads a digital signal across a wide range of frequencies. Because the signal is spread across a wider

---

[4] The ISM band is an unlicensed band centered on 2.4 GHz. The FCC dictates the use of either frequency-hopping spread spectrum (FHSS) or direct-sequence spread spectrum (DSSS) technology.

range of frequencies than required, it is less detectable and less susceptible to jamming. Spread spectrum modulation has always been considered ideal for military purposes because less energy is concentrated on any particular narrow-band channel.

## Code Division Multiple Access (CDMA)

Multiplexing refers to the technique of allowing multiple users to share a channel (i.e., multiple-access). It is a critical aspect of wireless communication. For a given band of frequencies, the multiplexing technology determines the number of users that can simultaneously operate. Thus, the multiplexing technology is one of the key elements driving bandwidth efficiency and network capacity.

CDMA is one of the key multiple access techniques used in wireless communication, with the others being TDMA[5] and frequency division multiple access (FDMA).[6] CDMA, as its name implies, describes schemes that use spread spectrum modulation, as well as codes, so that multiple users can share a frequency spectrum.

In CDMA, multiple users all transmit on the same channel at the same time, but transmissions avoid interference (and are differentiated) by the use of special codes that both the receiver and sender know. General advantages of CDMA include amelioration of multipath effects,[7] better spectrum utilization (frequency guard bands are voided), and good anti-jam performance.

---

[5] Time division multiplexing is a simple method to allocate transmission time between multiple users on a common channel. The Army's Enhanced Position Location Reporting System (EPLRS) is a TDMA system, i.e., users are preconfigured to transmit during a given timeslot, on a periodic basis.

[6] Frequency division multiplexing allocates a given communication channel among multiple users by giving dedicated frequency assignments to individual users. It can be convenient when there is a small, fixed number of users. It can become inefficient, in its most basic implementation, since spectral "guard" bands must be allocated between each of the subbands to prevent interference. This is not considered a scalable scheme.

[7] Multipath effects are a classic problem for wireless transmission. Wireless transmissions travel from a source to a destination and follow more than one path, as the signal can bounce off of objects. The same message can be received more than once when the direct, line-of-

CDMA can use frequency hopping (as does the Army's SINCGARS radio). Frequency hopping involves the coordinated switching of transmission frequency between various narrowband subchannels. In the commercial world, frequency hopping is now only being considered mainly for short, personal communication schemes like Bluetooth because it is less efficient (but it does require less power).

**O-CDMA versus DS-CDMA**

Frequency hopping aside, CDMA types can be differentiated by two types of coding schemes: orthogonal CDMA (O-CDMA) and direct sequence CDMA (DS-CDMA).

O-CDMA uses codes that are orthogonal,[8] meaning they have zero cross-correlation. This means that two transmitters using such codes will not interfere with each other as they transmit in the same frequency band. There is a limit to the number of orthogonal codes that can be generated. Hence there is a fixed limit to the number of users. Also, to achieve zero cross-correlation, perfect synchronization is required between the users. Thus there is a more limited set of applications for this to be practical.

The codes for DS-CDMA/DSSS are not orthogonal, and some amount of cross-correlation exists. This means there could be some interference between users in the same band. However, there isn't the same limit on the number of users as with O-CDMA.

**Direct Sequence Spread Spectrum (DSSS)**

The Army Spectrum Management Office (2002) provides a concise description of DSSS as follows:

> Direct Sequence Spread Spectrum (DSSS) is the most widely used form of spread spectrum. A DSSS signal is created by mul-

---

sight transmission arrives, followed by reflected signals, which arrive later and can potentially confuse the receiver.

[8] By definition, multiple users with an orthogonal set of codes can simultaneously transmit without interference.

tiplying an RF carrier with a very high bit-rate pseudo-noise (PN) digital signal. This modulation scheme causes the otherwise narrow band RF signal to be replaced with a very wide bandwidth signal with the spectral equivalent of a noise signal. The DSSS signals generated with this technique appear as noise in the frequency domain. The wide bandwidth provided by the PN code allows the signal power to drop below the noise threshold without loss of information . . . Spread Spectrum systems transmit an RF signal bandwidth that may be as wide as 20 to 254 times the bandwidth of the information being sent. Some special application spread spectrum systems that are designed to exhibit strong LPI and anti-jam characteristics employ RF bandwidths 1000 times their information bandwidth.

Note that the transmitter and receiver share the codes, so information broken up in this manner can be recovered.

### Orthogonal Frequency Division Multiplexing (OFDM)

One key principle behind OFDM is that the data stream is broken up into multiple lower-speed data streams or subcarriers. This is depicted in Figure A.2, taken from Yeung, Takai, and Bagrodia (2002). The figure diagrams how the data to be transmitted are converted into "a series of independent narrowband signals placed side-by-side in the frequency domain" with the subcarriers overlapping. The figure identifies the Fast Fourier Transform (FFT) and inverse FFT processors as the hardware components used to encode the data into subcarriers and to decode the data on the channel.

## Multipath Effects

The manner in which OFDM uses multiple subcarriers is one way to deal with "multipath effects." Multipath effects get worse as data rates get higher. To reiterate: OFDM essentially allows smaller bandwidth "pipes" to transmit larger amounts of data. For this reason, OFDM is considered a multicarrier communication technique. While there are

**Figure A.2**
**OFDM Process**

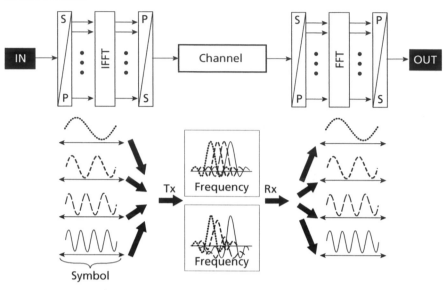

RAND *MG156-A.2*

SOURCE: Yeung, Takai, and Bagrodia (2002). Used with permission.

other techniques that use multiple carriers, OFDM can be made to be efficient by having these subcarriers overlap, as shown in Figure A.3, adapted from Chheda (2002).

This brings us to the other key principle behind OFDM: interference between subcarriers is still avoided because the subcarriers are made to be orthogonal to each other.

## Comparison of Types of OFDM

OFDM is to an extent a concept with many commercial names and/or variants. They are described in Table A.2. One of the newer commercial standards (802.11a) for higher-speed wireless networking incorporates OFDM.

**Figure A.3**
**OFDM Efficiency via Subcarrier Overlap**

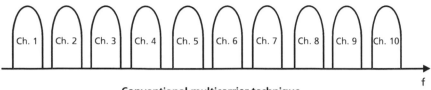

**Conventional multicarrier technique**

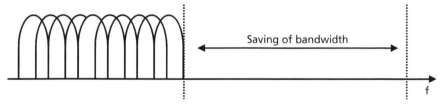

Saving of bandwidth

**Orthogonal multicarrier modulation technique**

RAND *MG156 A.3*

SOURCE: Chheda (2002).

## OFDM: Past, Present, and Future

OFDM was proposed over thirty years ago, but implementation issues plagued its development until recently. The JTRS (Cluster 1) intends to be OFDM capable (JTRS 2C is DSSS based). Northrup-Grumman and Flarion, Inc. have proposed using an OFDM variant (called flash-OFDM) in a proposal for a national emergency communication system, i.e., one that is mobile and can be trucked into an area (McHugh, 2002). Flarion claims it can reach near the lofty goals for 4G data rates (1 Gbps indoors and 100 Mbps outdoors) with its flash-OFDM approach. We have not seen data on this claim. Raytheon is testing a scheme called adaptive-vector OFDM that is designed to incorporate the use of adaptive antenna arrays with OFDM-capable radios.

**Table A.2**
**OFDM and OFDM-Inspired Types**

| Name | Description | Use | Notes |
|---|---|---|---|
| C-OFDM | Code OFDM | European digital radio and TV | |
| BST-OFDM | Band Segmented Transmission OFDM | Japanese digital TV | A more advanced version of C-OFDM that splits up signal into finer subchannels |
| W-OFDM | Wideband OFDM | Claimed by Wi-Lan, Inc. as proprietary version | Some argue that this proprietary scheme is similar to C-OFDM |
| Flash OFDM | Also known as frequency-hopping OFDM | Potential 4G standard | Flarion claims data rates 3–4 times commercial 3G goals;[a] Northrup-Grumman proposes a national emergency communication system using this technology. |
| V-OFDM | Vectored OFDM for fixed wireless using multiple antennas | | Corporate owner: Clarity Wireless and CISCO |
| AV-OFDM | Raytheon proposes a hybrid called Adaptive Vector OFDM; frequency-hopping hybrid of FDMA/CDMA/TDMA | | Raytheon concept claimed to be a hybrid |
| Multi-Carrier-CDMA | Rockwell Collins proposes a hybrid that combines aspects of frequency hopping, DSSS, and the multicarrier modulation inherent with OFDM to produce a more AL/LPD scheme relative to "simple OFDM" | | Part of FCS communication program |

[a] McHugh, Josh, "A High Wireless Act," *Redherring*, October 2002.

## BLAST

The Bell Labs Space and Time (BLAST) concept is a wireless communications technique that uses multi-element antennas at both transmitter and receiver. It has the potential for high spectral efficiency. It is not clear how such an arrangement is to be used in a mobile, tactical environment. The following description of BLAST was taken from www1.bell-labs.com/project/blast/:

> BLAST is an extraordinarily bandwidth-efficient approach to wireless communication which takes advantage of the spatial dimension by transmitting and detecting a number of independent co-channel data streams using multiple, essentially co-located, antennas. The central paradigm behind BLAST is the exploitation, rather than the mitigation, of multipath effects in order to achieve very high spectral efficiencies (bits/sec/Hz), significantly higher than are possible when multipath is viewed as an adversary rather than an ally. Using our laboratory testbed, the BLAST team recently demonstrated what we believe to be unprecedented wireless spectral efficiencies, ranging from 20–40 bps/Hz. By comparison, the efficiencies achieved using traditional wireless modulation techniques range from around 1–5 bps/Hz (mobile cellular) to around 10–12 bps/Hz (point-to-point fixed microwave systems). In the 30 kHz bandwidth utilized by our research testbed, the raw spectral efficiencies realized thus far in the lab correspond to payload data rates ranging from roughly 0.5 Mb/s to 1 Mb/s. By contrast, the data rate achievable in this bandwidth using typical traditional methods is only about 50 kbps.

## Hybrids

All of the schemes above have advantages and disadvantages. Hybrid, multicarrier schemes[9] (that utilize aspects of both CDMA and

---

[9] Linnartz and Hara (1996) provide historical background on multicarrier modulation in general as follows: "Multi-Carrier Modulation (MCM) is the principle of transmitting data by dividing the stream into several parallel bit streams, each of which has a much lower bit rate, and by using these substreams to modulate several carriers. The first systems using

OFDM) are likely to be the most advantageous ones. The term "Multicarrier CDMA" (MC-CDMA) is sometimes used to describe concepts that combine conventional CDMA and OFDM. A fairly comprehensive overview is provided by Hara and Prasad (1997). More research and development is probably needed for these concepts to get fielded.

## Wi-Fi5

"Wi-Fi5" is a moniker used by some to refer to the IEEE 802.11a standard for wireless networks. The standard was proposed earlier than Wi-Fi but is considered newer and is expected to achieve higher real-world throughputs. It is intended to operate commercially at 5 GHz, hence the name "Wi-Fi5."

The related IEEE 802.11g standard is a mix of the two standards described above. It is intended to be used at the 2.4 Ghz, as with the "b" standard, and hence it will be compatible with the "b" standard. But it utilizes OFDM, as does the "a" standard. Its stated maximum throughput will be at least as good as the "a" standard (10–11 Mbps). Thus, 802.11g is related to Wi-Fi and Wi-Fi5.

Estimates of real-world maximum throughput are roughly one-third to one-half the stated maximum. These estimates are documented in Dornan (2002):

> The theoretical maximum capacity of 802.11b is 11 MBps, which is often quoted by vendors and by groups such as WECA. It pushes wireless LANs through an important psychological

---

MCM were military HF radio links in the late 1950s and early 1960s. Orthogonal Frequency Division Multiplexing (OFDM), a special form of MCM with densely spaced subcarriers and overlapping spectra was patented in the U.S. in 1970. OFDM time-domain waveforms are chosen such that mutual orthogonality is ensured even though subcarrier spectra may overlap. It appeared that such waveforms can be generated using a Fast Fourier Transform at the transmitter and receiver. For a relatively long time, the practicality of the concept appeared limited . . . today we appear to be on the verge of a breakthrough of MCM techniques. Many of the implementation problems appear."

barrier, matching the speed of the original Ethernet standard. However, the number is misleading. It refers to the total physical layer capacity, much of which is used by the protocol itself, so it is not actually available for data. The maximum data rate of an 802.11b network is really [at best] only about 6Mbps, and that can be achieved only under optimum condition—over a short range and with no interference. It quickly drops when packet collisions or other errors occur. A 50% error rate will reduce the real-throughput by about two thirds, to only 2Mbps.

## Ultra-Wideband Technologies

The term "wideband" in the communication vernacular refers to a system that uses a very wide range of frequencies. Ultra-wideband technology (UWB)[10] involves radios that transmit across a very large part of the spectrum, perhaps as much as 2 GHz. In this manner, it is similar to the spread spectrum concept. An important detail for the commercial application of UWB technology is its low power feature. The idea is that power is distributed across this very wide band such that the amount of power transmitted at any narrowband in the range is small and does not interfere with other radio transmissions. This can allow this technology to be very spectral efficient. Critics of the commercial application of this technology question the claim of low interference with other technologies. It is important to note that commercial applications focus on short-range communications, e.g., 10 meters or less.

A key advantage of the UWB concept is that simple pulses can be used to transmit information (almost like Morse code). The combination of low power and less complexity could mean less cost. From this perspective, it is a competitor to Bluetooth technologies. Table A.3 contains a comparison of UWB to other concepts like Bluetooth and Wi-Fi. On February 14, 2002, the Federal Communi-

---

[10] The concept has been around in military labs since the 1960s, mainly for radar systems that can look for objects buried below ground and behind walls (Jonietz, 2002).

cations Commission (FCC) authorized the commercial deployment of UWB technology (see www.uwb.org).

Edwards (2001) explains how UWB could facilitate useful characteristics for the military communications with respect to covertness, jam-resistance, and resistance to multipath interference:

> Ultra-wideband signals are spread across a larger band of frequencies than is required for normal narrowband transmissions. As a result, the average power or amplitude at any given frequency is virtually indistinguishable from background noise. This makes UWB signals more covert than narrowband signals. The wide operating bands of UWB systems make it difficult for jammers to distribute enough energy across all used frequencies (up to several GHz in some cases). Ultra-wideband signals also do not fade as much because they are time-modulated rather than amplitude modulated or frequency modulated. UWB radio pulses are short of such duration that the reflected versions of the signal do not cause destructive interference.

For the reasons described above, military communication applications of this technology are being pursued by DARPA, which has initiated a new program called NETEX (Networking in Extreme Environments). The goal of the program is to demonstrate "ultra-wideband wireless networking capability that will enable us to communicate with troops inside buildings, in built-up areas, and in other challenging environments" (Freebersyser, 2002, quotation attributed to Steven P. Griggs). DARPA intends to examine interference issues with other types of radios.

## Antenna Technologies

Directional antennas are being proposed to address key areas of improvement needed in both the commercial and military sectors. Potential benefits include (1) better energy savings, (2) reduced interference, and (3) potential for improved throughput/capacity. Directional antennas can potentially provide improvements in these

**Table A.3**
**Comparisons of Selected Wireless Communication Technologies**

| Technology | Range (meters) | Data Rate (Mbps) | Power (milliwatts) | Best Suited for | Commercial Availability |
|---|---|---|---|---|---|
| Ultra-wideband | 10 | 100 | 200 (peak) | Short-range, high-speed data transfer (such as wireless video and audio) | Unclear |
| 802.11a | 50 | 30 | 1,000–2,000 | High-speed wireless computer networks | Now |
| 802.11b | 100 | 6 | 500 | Computer networking and Internet access | Now |
| Bluetooth [a] | 10 | 1 | 30 | Connecting computing devices over short distances for text transfer | Now |

[a] Bluetooth is a short-range communication concept suited for wireless connections of peripherals. See http://www.bluetooth.com.

areas, in addition to improved information assurance, i.e., low probability of intercept (LPI), Anti-Jam (AJ), and low probability of detection (LPD).

## Antenna Types

We can define two general categories of antennas: omnidirectional and directional. Most commercial wireless local area networks rely on omnidirectional antennas, i.e., antennas that transmit in all directions. Antennas designed to be pointed in a particular direction are called directional antennas.

Directional antennas can have a wide beamwidth, e.g., 120 degrees, or a very narrow one, e.g., 30 degrees or less. The gain for directional antennas can be relatively high, but the penalty is that they have to be mechanically or electronically pointed and arrayed to ensure the ability to transmit/receive in selective directions.

Steered beam antennas are a type of directional antenna designed to change their beam pattern via software control, not physical positioning as with other types of directional antennas (see Figure A.4).

## Transmission Energy Savings

Energy efficiency is important for nodes in military wireless networks for a variety of reasons. One reason is to reduce onboard energy consumption on vehicles and man-packs that may rely on battery power at least part of the time.[11] Another is the reduction in interference that is engendered when a data packet is transmitted with the least power necessary to get to its intended receiver; in this manner, greater "spatial reuse" is facilitated (Vaidya, 2001). Spyropoulos and Raghav-

---

[11] While onboard generators power most devices in Army combat vehicles, there are most likely instances in which it is desirable to have devices powered using batteries instead of an engine. In fact, future tactical vehicles are envisioned to be hybrids (i.e., battery power supports propulsion power needs). Battery life then becomes an issue and, thus, the energy use of communication systems.

**Figure A.4**
**Steered Beam Antennas**

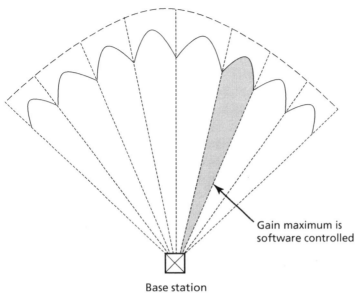

Gain maximum is
software controlled

Base station

RAND *MG156-A.4*

endra (2002) show a 45 percent improvement in energy cost savings
when directional antennas are used instead of omnidirectional ones.

## MAC and Routing Protocols for Directional Antennas

Research and development of MAC[12] and routing protocols for directional antennas is underway. Srisathapornphat and Shen (2003)
document a few efforts. MAC protocols for some omnidirectional
antennas rely on broadcasts of request-to-send (RTS), clear-to-send
(CTS), and acknowledgments of successful transmissions. These
overhead messages, which are not the data that need to be communi-
cated, are broadcast to reserve access to the channel for the data. Ex-
cessive overhead messages are wasteful but likely when the network is

---

[12] MAC, or medium access control, refers to a methodology that determines how different
users on a network share the same resources.

mobile and constantly changing. More research is needed on routing protocols for directional antennas, as existing commercial systems (for wireless LANs) assume omnidirectional use. Selected routing protocols are surveyed in Appendix B.

## Summary and Observation

This appendix surveyed advanced technologies relevant to the Army. Efforts highlighted include those being pursued in the commercial world as well as those being developed in academia and government laboratories. It is not clear where the commercial world will be in 10 or more years;[13] however, it is unlikely that it will develop something other than the current infrastructure-based 2G and 3G mobile phone system. The Army wants to adopt a communication architecture that is mobile, ad hoc, and infrastructureless. Certainly, this is advantageous for the warfighter. But any acquisition advantage gained from leveraging commercial technologies could fail to materialize.

---

[13] Karen Miller, "Is Wi-Fi Just a Bubble," *Newsweek*, September 29, 2003.

# Routing Protocols for MANETs

Data routes in mobile ad hoc networks must be discovered. The effect of mobile nodes on routing can be profound, since overhead associated with route discovery can be significant compared with a fixed network. A number of routing algorithms have been developed to deal with the mobility aspect. Routing protocols for MANETs are being investigated heavily at the university research level (although the vast majority of efforts are focused on protocols that assume omnidirectional antennas). A large number of specific proposals for protocols have been proposed in the Internet Engineering Task Force (IETF). A subset is described in Table B.1.

Investigation and comparison of various protocols is still an active area of research. There may exist a protocol yet to be developed that is ideal for tactical MANETs. In particular, more investigation of routing protocols for directional antennas is needed.

Feeney (1999) suggests a taxonomy based on the following:

- Scheduling and route information maintenance: proactive and reactive types.
- State information: how informed each node is of the whereabouts of others.
- Structure: uniform or nonuniform (hierarchical) types of nodes.
- Communication model (single or multiple channels).

## Route Maintenance

Routing protocols fall into two general categories: proactive and reactive. There are conflicting results on which is better. Perhaps the answer is neither, since the correct choice is situation dependent. Perhaps the answer is both, since they can be combined as a hybrid. The pros and cons for these approaches are described in the following paragraphs.

Proactive protocols require nodes to constantly assess source-destination routes and thus "suffer the disadvantage of additional control traffic that is needed to continually update stale routes" (Perkins, 2001, p. 7). In general, the maintenance of proactive routing information can be costly in a wireless, ad hoc network. Sánchez, Evans, and Minden (1999) provide reasonable conjecture on this particular class of routing protocols: "In highly dynamic networks, it is futile to provide support for routing protocols that continuously evaluate routes within the network before they are actually requested (i.e., pro-active protocols). Pro-active techniques may cause tremendous traffic overheads on evaluating unnecessary routes. But routing procedures that work on an as needed basis (i.e., reactive protocols) are more suitable to large, highly dynamic (MANETs)."

"On-demand" or reactive protocols develop routes when requested as opposed to proactive protocols[1] that develop routes constantly. Reactive protocols are designed so routing information is acquired only when actually needed. However, the delay to find a route may be intolerable. Reactive protocols may often use far less network capacity for maintaining the route tables at each node, but the latency for many applications will drastically increase (Perkins, 2001, pp. 7–8). Some results suggest that this approach, used in commercial wireless networks, could also lead to significant overhead in mobile ad hoc networks.

---

[1] Note: Proactive protocols are also called "table-driven" protocols, since each node has to maintain tables of information on how to route to any node in the network.

Hybrid protocols that are sometimes reactive and sometimes proactive are highly advantageous. One example is the Zone Routing Protocol (ZRP). According to Perkins (2001),

> The Zone Routing Protocol takes a fresh yet time-tested approach to protocol improvement by constructing a way to hybridize table-driven protocols (such as DSDV) with on-demand protocols. ZRP uses zones that are similar to clusters, but instead of hierarchical routing between clusters being used, special border nodes are dynamically selected that connect adjacent zones. A zone radius parameter dynamically adjusts the size of the zone, in terms of the number of hops, as the network topology changes. A different routing protocol can be used between zones as compared to the one used within a zone. A proactive scheme is used inside the zone. Outside the zone routes are discovered only reactively. This approach is almost guaranteed to find a happy medium between the two extremes that exhibits improved properties.

## State Information

Some protocols require each node to maintain "large-scale topological information" such that neighboring nodes must advertise their connectivity to each other on a regular basis. This is referred to as a link-state approach, where "each node maintains a view of the network topology with a cost for each link . . . each node periodically broadcasts the link costs of its outgoing links to all other nodes [via] flooding" (Perkins, 2001, p. 55). This can be expensive in terms of overhead and thus scales poorly. An alternative is having nodes maintain/exchange more basic information with its immediate neighbors, i.e., distance and direction. A noteworthy approach is called Hazy-Sighted Link State (HSLS) routing. This is a hybrid scheme proposed by BBN that claims to be the proper balance between the need to reduce overhead traffic while maintaining up-to-date routing information in a mobile network. Nodes send out updates (of routing information) to nearby nodes frequently and to farther out nodes less often. The idea is that if links change their state frequently, only the most recent change is disseminated. Messages are routed using the accurate local information, and as the messages become closer to their destination, the route information becomes more accurate.

## Structure

Protocols may be hierarchical in that some nodes serve as backbones or cluster-heads. Others treat all nodes as common. The latter are referred to as flat networks. Hierarchical routing protocols are quite different from routing protocols for purely flat networks.

The taxonomy utilized by Grossman and Portnoy (n.d.) is taken from IETF submissions and describes a number of the proposed routing protocols with more detail than the taxonomy suggested by Feeney (1999).

- **Loop freedom.** Loops in routes can easily lead to packets' floating around in a mobile network, hogging bandwidth and never reaching the intended recipient.
- **Multiple routes.** Calculation of multiple routes from source to recipient.
- **Unidirectional link support.** Nodes' ability to send messages to other nodes without a need for acknowledgement.
- **Quality of service support.** Whether or not guarantees on network performance can be facilitated.
- **Periodic broadcasts.** Reflects whether or not a protocol will be required on broadcasts to all nodes.
- **Sequenced data.** Reflects whether the protocol required sequenced data transmission.

Table B.1 lists a host of protocols. But the number of these protocols suitable for tactical MANETs is much smaller, since few have been tested for a tactical environment. Still, if directional antennas are planned, perhaps none of the above are usable. Clearly, research and development on routing protocols needs to continue.

**Table B.1**
**Routing Protocols in Development and/or Proposed**

|  | DSDV | DSR | TORA | ZRP | CBRP | OLSR | AODV | STAR | CEDAR | RDMAR |
|---|---|---|---|---|---|---|---|---|---|---|
| Loop-free | Y | Y | N | Y | Y | Y | Y | N | Y | Y |
| Multiple routes | N | Y | Y | N | Y | Y | N | Y | Y | Y |
| Reactive | N | Y | Y | Part | Y | N | Y | N | Part | Y |
| Unidirectional link support | N | N | N | N | Y | N | N | Y | N | Y |
| QoS support | N | N | N | N | N | N | N | N | Y | N |
| Multicast | N | N | N | N | N | N | Y | N | N | N |
| Security | N | N | N | N | N | N | N | N | N | N |
| Periodic broadcast | Y | N | Y | Y | Y | Y | Y | N | Y | N |
| Sequenced data | N | N | Y | N | N | N | N | N | N | N |

# Who's Working the Problem and Emerging Concepts

A large number of organizations are addressing FCS communications and sharing information. We describe some of them and the concepts they are exploring.

## DARPA

### FCS Communications Program
The FCS Communications Program is developing and testing hardware and software for mobile ad hoc networks, using directional antennas, with both terrestrial and airborne nodes. Sass and Freebersyser (2002) summarize the motivation for the program as follows.

> In the frequency bands generally used for tactical mobile operations (30–250MHz), there is generally not adequate bandwidth available to provide both increased capacity and AJ/LPD. As a result, at the onset of this new DARPA program, it was concluded that a "high band" RF system, one operating above the microwave band, would be required to supplement the lower band RF systems traditionally used for tactical operations. Furthermore, since both their smaller platform dimensions and their required mobility will restrict the size of the antenna structures for FCS platforms, the selection of the frequency of the high band system became a critical decision (trading antenna gain, propagation characteristics, technology maturity, and spectrum availability). It was concluded that the selection of a frequency band around 38 GHz would enable the simultaneous achieve-

ment of high data rates, LPD, AJ, and mobile operation through the use of highly directional antennas. A low band system would still be necessary for interoperability with conventional ground forces and for operation in environments where a direct line of sight may be unavailable due to terrain, foliage, or weather. Providing the ability to transmit large amounts of data quickly while avoiding jamming and detection will require significant advancements in transmitters, receivers, and directional antenna technology, as well as the use of mobile, ad hoc networking techniques with directional antennas.

Among the specific projects associated with the DARPA FCS program is an effort called Utilizing Directional Antennas for Ad hoc Networking (UDAAN). Quoting Sass and Freebersyser (2002), this project is

> a DARPA-sponsored project under the FCS Communications program. BBN Technologies, Stow Research LLC, and Texas A&M University (TAMU) are developing a suite of protocols for utilizing directional antennas in ad hoc networks. A significant payoff from UDAAN will be increased effective capacity. Other payoffs include decreased packet latency, increased connectivity, greater multicast efficiency, and lower probability of detection/interference.

> [The] contention is that the directionality inherent in high gain antennas can significantly improve the performance of ad hoc networks by delivering higher effective capacity, lower latency, robust connectivity, and enhanced security.

Table C.1 highlights other DARPA FCS Communications Program funded initiatives. Several demonstrations have highlighted the successful integration of a number of the technologies and concepts outlined in the table. The latest demonstration (Demo 3) was in August 2003 at the Orchard Training Area near Boise, Idaho. The tests involved 20 ground-based vehicles (SUVs, one M-113A, one HMMVV) and up to seven airborne nodes (two helicopters with sling nodes acting as airborne nodes and up to five UAVs). The

**Table C.1**
**DARPA FCS Communications Program Funded Initiatives**

| Vendor | Topic | Description |
|---|---|---|
| Rockwell-Collins | (OFDM) digital receiver architecture | Develop a broadband waveform that meets the multi-rate FCS communications requirements and is expandable, reconfigurable, and JTRS-compliant that utilizes OFDM. |
| BBN | Protocols for directional antennas | Develop network and MAC layer protocols for the exploitation of directional antennas to provide network performance improvements in capacity, latency, robustness, and security. |
| Lucent Technologies | BLAST: Bell Labs layered space time processing | Provide high-data-rate communications using non-line-of-sight links in heavy scattering environments with mobile end points. |
| Raytheon | Bandwidth-efficient networking with beam forming antennas | Develop network and media access control (MAC) protocols that exploit directional antennas and node-tracking data and will demonstrate ad hoc networking with directional antennas in simulation and prototypes; investigate techniques for rapid beam-forming and denial of service prevention. |
| Rockwell-Collins | High-band, 38-gigahertz, beam-former, active-array antenna | Develop active array antenna to enable efficient beam-steering. |
| TRW | Mobile, wideband, millimeter-wave radio | Develop 100 megabits per second, peer-to-peer communication radio with extreme anti-jam, low probability of intercept and low probability of deception. |
| Raytheon | Smart antennas and software radio for FCS low bands | Develop and demonstrate a smart, reconfigurable antenna, a JTRS-compliant Ultra Comm software-defined radio, and an adaptive vector OFDM high-data-rate waveform. |
| Scalable Network Technology Inc. | Network simulation | A high-fidelity, scalable, network simulation (e.g., GloMoSim) based on the QualNet tool that allows detailed modeling of each layer of the communications stack and demonstrates real-time simulation of networks with hundreds of nodes. |
| BAE Systems | Low band arch. system for directional antennas | Develop an ultra-wideband, co-located, meanderline antenna and associated siting (platform integration) techniques. |

SOURCE: DARPA Fact Sheet, "Future Combat Systems Communications Program," May 2001. See also http://www.darpa.mil/body/ NewsItems/wordfiles/FCSComms501.doc.

ground vehicles moved on two roads and airborne nodes flew to provide connectivity. Also deployed were Unattended Ground Sensors (UGS) to provide radar, SIGINT, and IR data that were fed into the communication network. The SUVs used directional antennas to give redundant 20 degree antenna patterns. Robotic vehicles were employed.

### DARPA Next Generation (XG) Communications Program

The XG Communications Program is intended to demonstrate enabling technologies and system concepts to improve spectral utilization of military radio frequency emitters by a factor of 20. These demonstrations will include demonstrating a low power/wideband spectrum sensor, time/frequency agile waveforms, and dynamic spectrum access and control. Stated program goals: demonstrate an appliqué for legacy and future emitter systems for joint service utility; develop enabling technologies and system concepts to provide assured military communications and sensors in support of worldwide, short-notice deployments through the dynamic redistribution of allocated spectrum; provide a common technical architecture that can meet the needs of both military and civilian future (beyond 3G) mobile communications systems.

Quoting Price (2003):

> Development of spectrum efficient technologies is a key component of any spectrum management solution. We are moving forward in developing what we consider to be the cutting edge of spectrum use: DARPA's neXt Generation spectrum program, known as XG. XG capitalizes on one of the factors identified by the FCC Spectrum Task Force: access to spectrum is the key limiting factor in using spectrum. In other words, spectrum may be available but there is no way to access it. XG will allow the dynamic management of spectrum use by defining access based on the dimensions of time, frequency and location. Current spectrum users routinely differentiate on the basis of frequency and location only. Enabling spectrum users to differentiate on the basis of time will allow more users to access the spectrum. This will help change the antiquated zero-sum characteristics of current spectrum allocations. When XG and other technological

initiatives come to fruition, it will allow us move from a "use rights model" of spectrum use, to a "dynamic access model." This will be good for our military, other government users, and industry.

### Networking In Extreme Environments (NETEX)

The DARPA NETEX program is focused on communications for urban and special operations. The program "aims to create new wireless networking technologies that address the challenges of rapidly creating robust networks in complex and hostile environments, and of coordinating the assignment of available spectrum." Specifically, ultra-wideband communication (see Appendix A) technologies and its networking capability are being investigated.

### Tera Hertz Operational Reachback (THOR)

The DARPA THOR program is focused on providing "flexible broadband connectivity" to any point on the globe. This will involve optical links from airborne platforms down to the ground as well as other air-to-air and ground-to-air links to enable communication with CONUS from the theatre and back.

### Adaptive C4ISR Node

The DARPA adaptive C4ISR node (ACN) program is focused on providing "a multi-mission RF system that provides seamless interoperable communications, simultaneously with SIGINT, EW, and IO capabilities."

## CECOM, ARL, and ARO

CECOM, ARL, and ARO are developing technologies for mobile ad hoc networking. An example is the CERDEC Multifunctional On-the-Move Secure Adaptive Integrated Communications (MOSAIC) program.

## MOSAIC

According to the Army budget justification (Army, 2002), MOSAIC is an advanced technology demonstration that will "provide the communications technology foundation that seamlessly and automatically supports secure, high volume, multimedia traffic in a dispersed OTM network." The stated goal is to "provide the Army's Objective Force with distributed, mobile, secure, self-organizing communications networks." As depicted in Figure C.1, the program intends to demonstrate (1) ad hoc networking, (2) quality of service protocols to enable multiple classes of traffic to share network resources, and (3) vertical and horizontal network hand-off mechanisms to support airborne-node/SATCOM utilization.

### Communication and Network Collaborative Technology Alliance

The Army Research Laboratory (ARL) sponsors a communications and network alliance with twelve university and industry consortium

**Figure C.1**
**MOSAIC Envisions UAV/SATCOM Utilization for Mobile Nodes**

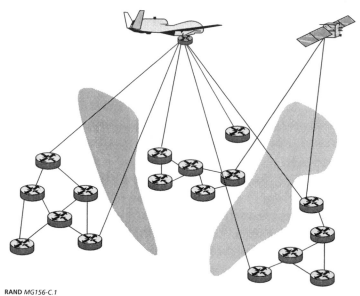

members.[1] The objective of the alliance is to study "technologies that enable a fully-mobile, fully-communicating, agile, situation-aware, and survivable lightweight force with internetted C4ISR systems." Specific research objectives and technologies include:

- survivable wireless mobile networks;
- signal processing techniques to enable reliable low-power multimedia communications among highly mobile nodes;
- secure jam-resistant communications;
- tactical information protection technologies that are real-time.

## Others

CECOM/Mitre/TRAC is developing a communications networking architecture also, approaching the problem from a top-down look based on postulated operational scenarios. AMSAA is currently using NETWARS, a Joint Staff communications model, to assess FCS bandwidth needs. The Lead System Integrator (Boeing/SAIC) for FCS is developing its own system and operational architecture. ASD/C3I is addressing bandwidth issues at the tactical level (using the JTRS as discussed previously) and in its TCA (defined earlier), which is developing a concept for very high speed terrestrial and satellite communications for global connectivity.

---

[1] Telecordia (lead), BAE, Network Associates, Motorola, BBN, Georgia Tech, University of Maryland, University of Delaware, Princeton, Johns Hopkins University, Morgan State University, CCNY, and Clark Atlanta University.

# References

Anderson, C., "Transformational Communications," MILSATCOM Joint Program Office, March 2002.

*Army Communicator,* "TSM Update," Winter 2002, pp. 27–29.

Army Research Laboratory, "Short-range UHF Wireless Communications for Unattended Battlefield Sensors: An Initial Site Evaluation to Characterize Propagation Across Forested Terrain," SPIE, April 2002.

Army Spectrum Management Office, "Frequency & Band Selection Guidance for Objective Force (OF) Managers and Developers," February 4, 2002.

Banica, I., and C. Vladeanu, "Performance of Iterative Multistage Detectors for DS-CDMA Systems," IEEE International Conference on Telecommunications' IEEE ICT2001', Proceedings, Vol. 3, pp. 35–39, Bucuresti, Iunie 4–7, 2001.

Blazevic, Ljubica, and Jean-Yves Le Boudec and Silvia Giordano, "A Location Based Routing Method for Irregular Mobile Ad Hoc Networks," accessed at citeseer.nj.nec.com/blazevic03location.html, 2003.

Bridges, Andrew, "Pentagon Turns to Commercial Satellites to Ease War Data Squeeze," Associated Press, March 27, 2003.

Casper, Lawrence E., et al., "Knowledge-based Warfare: A Security Strategy for the Next Century," *Joint Forces Quarterly* 13, Autumn 1996, pp. 81–89.

Cebrowski, Arthur K., and John J. Garstka, "Network-centric Warfare: Its Origin and Future," Naval Institute *Proceedings,* January 1998.

Chheda, Shital Ratilal, "A Comparison Between Synchronous CDMA and Orthogonal Frequency Division Multiplexing (OFDM) for Fixed Broadband Wireless Access," Master's Thesis, Department of Electrical and Computer Engineering, Virginia Tech, 2002.

CIS Division, NATO C3 Agency, "The NATO Post-2000 Narrow Band Voice Coder: Test and Selection of STANAG 4591, Technical Presentation-001.

Congressional Budget Office, "The Army's Bandwidth Bottleneck," August 2003.

Das, S., C. Perkins, and E. Royer, "Performance Comparison of Two On-demand Routing Protocols for Ad-hoc Networks," INFOCOM, 2000.

Department of Energy, Atmospheric Radiation Measurement Program, "Vaisala Ceilometer (Model CT25K)," accessed at http://www.arm.gov/docs.

Dornan, Andy, *The Essential Guide to Wireless Communications Applications*, Prentice Hall, 2002.

Edwards, Sean, *Freeing Mercury's Wings: Improving Tactical Communication in Cities*, Santa Monica, CA: RAND Corporation, MR-1316-A, 2001.

ElBatt, T.A., S.V. Krishnamurthy, D. Connors, and S. Dao, "Power Management for Throughput Enhancement in Wireless Ad-hoc Networks," Proceedings of the International Conference on Communications (ICC 2000), Volume 3, 2000, pp. 1506–1513.

"Encyclopedia of the Atmospheric Environment," http://www.doc.mmu.ac.uk/aric/eae/Weather/Older/Thunderstorms.html, Atmosphere, Climate and Environment Information Program.

Feeney, Laura M., "A Taxonomy for Routing Protocols in Mobile Ad-Hoc Networks," SICS Technical Report T99/07, October 1999, accessed at http://citeseer.nj.nec.com/feeney99taxonomy.html.

Foschini, G., and M. Gans, "On Limits of Wireless Communication in a Fading Environment When Using Multiple Antennas," submitted for publication, 1998, accessed at citeseer.nj.nec.com/foschini98limit.html.

Freebersyser, James, "ATO Communications," presented at the DARPA-Tech 2002 Conference, Anaheim, California, August 2, 2002. See also http://www.darpa.mil/DARPATech2002/presentation.html.

Freebersyser, James, and Berry Leiner, *A DoD Perspective on Mobile Ad-Hoc Networks, Ad-Hoc Networking*, Addison Wesley, 2001, ISBN 0-201-30976-9.

Graves, J.E., and S. Drenker, "Advancing Free Space Optical Communications with Adaptive Optics," http://www.aoptix.com/technology/white_papers/advancing_free_space.pdf.

Grobmeier, Col. John, PM TRACS, "Trends and Applications in Commercial Wireless Information Systems: Enabling FCS and U.S. Army OF," presented at AFCEA, Monmouth Chapter, 2002, accessed at http://www.afcea-ftmonmouth.org/documents/part%203.pdf.

Grossglauser, M., and D. Tse, "Mobility Increases the Capacity of Ad-hoc Wireless Networks," Conference Proceedings, IEEE, Volume 3, 2001, pp. 1360–1369.

Grossman, Daniel, and William Portnoy, "Ad-Hoc Routing for Mobile Packet Networks: A Literature Review," unpublished, accessed at http://www.cs.washington.edu/homes/grossman/projects/561projects/adhoc/adhoc.ps.

Gupta, P., and P. Kumar, "Capacity of Wireless Networks," Technical Report, University of Illinois, Urbana-Champaign, 1999.

Gupta, P., and P. Kumar, "The Capacity of Wireless Networks," *IEEE Transactions on Information Theory*, Vol. 46, No. 2, March 2000, available at http://www-ece.rice.edu/~amlexa/sensornets/gupta_kumar00.pdf.

Gupta, P., and P. Kumar, "Internets in the Sky: The Capacity of Three Dimensional Wireless Networks," *Communications in Information and Systems*, Vol. 1, No. 1, 2001, pp. 39–49.

Gupta, P., R. Gray, and P. Kumar, "An Experimental Scaling Law for Ad-hoc Networks," Technical Report, University of Illinois at Urbana, May, 2001, accessed at citeseer.nj.nec.com/gupta01experimental.html.

Hara, S., and R. Prasad, "Overview of Multicarrier CDMA," *IEEE Communications Magazine*, Vol. 35, No. 12, December 1997, pp. 126–133.

Haven, John, "Transformational Communication," presented at MILSAT 2003, February 2003, accessed at www.ags-inc.us/downloads/presentations/ColHaven_USAF.pdf.

Helmy, A., "Small Large-Scale Wireless Networks: Mobility-Assisted Resource Directory," U.S.*C-TR* and *ACM-LANL-NCSTRL*, July 2002.

Helmy, A., "Small Worlds in Wireless Networks," *IEEE Communications Letters*, Vol. 7, No. 12, October 2003.

Hillman, J., S. Jones, R. Nichols, and I. Wang, "Communications Network Architectures for the Army Future Combat System and Objective Force," Conference Proceedings, IEEE MILCOM, 2002.

Holland, Gavin, and Nitin H. Vaidya, "Analysis of {TCP} Performance Over Mobile Ad-Hoc Networks," *Mobile Computing and Networking*, 1999, pp. 219–230.

Horne, William D., "Adaptive Spectrum Access: Using the Full Spectrum Space," 31st Research Conference on Communication, Information and Internet Policy (TPRC), September 19, 2003.

Howard, William, "Coping with Change: Managing RF Spectrum to Meet DoD Needs," Report of the Defense Science Board Task Force on DoD Frequency Spectrum Issues, November 2000.

IEEE Infocom, "On-demand Routing Protocols for Ad-hoc Networks," Proceedings, March 2000.

Jain, Vivek, "Enhancing Network Throughput in Wireless Ad hoc Networks using Smart Antennas," 2003, accessed at http://www.ececs.uc.edu/~dlal/GM.ppt.

Jeganathan, D.M. and D.P. Ionov, "Multi-Gigabits-per-second Optical Wireless Communications," http://www.freespaceoptic.com/WhitePapers/Jeganathan%20%20(Optical%20Crossing).pdf.

Johns Hopkins University/Applied Physics Laboratory, Future Combat Systems Network-Centric Concepts and Operations, Phase I Report, May 2001.

Johns Hopkins University/Applied Physics Laboratory, Network-Centric Architectures for the Army Future Combat Systems and Objective Force Phase II: Architecture Performance Assessment, JWR-02-004, February 2002.

Joint Forces Command, "Global Information Grid Capstone Requirements Document," JROCM 134-01, August 2001.

Jonietz, Erika, "Ultra-wideband Squeezes In," *Technology Review*, September 2002, pp. 71–79.

Karn, P., "MACA: A New Channel Access Method for Packet Radio," in ARRL/CRRL Amateur Radio 9th Computer Networking Conference, pp. 134–140, ARRL, 1990.

Kim, I., and E. Korevarr, "Availability of Free Space Optics (FSO) and Hybrid FSO/RF Systems," accessed at www.freespaceoptic.com/ WhitePapers/SPIE2001b.pdf, Optical Access Incorporated, 2001.

Kim, I., B. McArthur, and E. Korevaar, "Comparison of Laser Beam Propagation at 785 nm and 1550 nm in Fog and Haze for Optical Wireless Communications," White Paper, Optical Access Incorporated, accessed at www.freespaceoptics.com, 2001.

Krane, Jim, "Military Wireless Networks Moving into Civilian Use," Associated Press, December 8, 2002.

Li, J., C. Blake, D. De Couto, H. Lee, and R. Morris, "Capacity of Ad-hoc Wireless Networks," *Mobile Computing and Networking*, 2001, pp. 61–69.

Linnartz, Jean-Paul, and Shinsuke Hara, "Special Issue on Multi-Carrier Modulation," *Wireless Personal Communication,* No. 1–2, 1996, http:// www.eecs.berkeley.edu/Research/Projects/ofdm/wireless/mcm.html.

Martin, Gary, "Open Architecture Solutions for Tactical Wireless Communication, Software Defines Radio Forum General Meeting, February 7, 2001, accessible at http://www.mmitsforum.org/ MTGS/mtg_22_feb01.

McHugh, Josh, "A High Wireless Act," *Redherring,* October 2002.

MILCOM, Communications for Network-Centric Operations, Creating the Information Force, Proceedings of MILCOM 2001, October 2001.

Milgram, S., "The Small World Problem," *Psychology Today*, Vol. 1, No. 61, 1967.

Moseley, Michael, "Operation Iraqi Freedom—By The Numbers," U.S.CENTAF, Assessment and Analysis Division, April 20, 2003 (unclassified).

Nasipuri, A., S. Ye, J. You, and R. Hiromotoe, "A MAC Protocol for Mobile Ad-hoc Networks Using Directional Antennas," IEEE, 2000.

National Telecommunications and Information Administration (NTIA), "An Assessment of the Viability of Accommodating Advanced Mobile Wireless (3G) Systems in the 1710–1770 MHz and 2110–2170 MHz

Bands," July 22, 2002, accessed on September 6, 2002 at http://www. ntia.doc.gov/ntiahome/threeg/va7222002/3Gva072202web.htm

Ohira, T., "Emerging Adaptive Antenna Techniques for Wireless Ad-hoc Networks," *The 2001 IEEE International Symposium on Circuits and Systems*, Vol. 4, May 6–9, 2001, pp. 858–861.

OSD/PA&E, "Communications and Digitization—The Communications Bottleneck," briefing, September 20, 2000.

Patch, Kimberly, "Shortcuts Lighten Wireless Load," TRN News, August 21–28, 2002, accessed at http://trnmag.com/Stories/2002/082102/ Shortcuts_lighten_wireless_load_082102.html on September 1, 2002.

Perkins, Charles (ed.), *Ad Hoc Networking*, Boston: Addison-Wesley, 2001.

Plummer, Ann, "Enduring Freedom Used Seven Times the Bandwidth Required in 1991 War," *Inside the Pentagon*, January 16, 2003.

Price, Stephen, Prepared Testimony to the Commercial Spectrum Enhancement Act Subcommittee on Telecommunications and the Internet, U.S. House of Representatives, March 25, 2003, accessed at energycommerce.house.gov/108/Hearings/03252003hearing843/Price1390.htm.

Rafol, S.D.B., and K. Wilson, "Adaptive Multiplexing for Free-Space Optical Communication: Wavelength- and Code-division Multiplexing Would Be Utilized for Security and Improved Performance," NASA Jet Propulsion Laboratory, accessed at http://www.nasatech.com/TSP/ PDFTSP/NPO20890.pdf.

Ramanathan, Ram, "Part 5: System Design, Prototype, and Experiences," Tutorial Session, Mobihoc'03, 2003, accessed at http://www.ir.bbn.com/ ~ramanath/tut-part5.pdf.

Reed, David, "How Wireless Networks Scale: The Illusion of Spectrum Scarcity," presented at FCC Technical Advisory Council, Washington, D.C., April 26, 2002.

Romero, Simon, "Military Now Often Enlists Commercial Technology," *The New York Times*, March 10, 2003.

Sanchez, Fabio, and Geraldo Chowell-Puente, "Disease Dynamics On a Small-World and Other Network," Technical Report, Cornell University, August 27, 2001.

Sanchez, M., "Multiple Access Protocols with Smart Antennas in Multihop Ad Hoc Rural-Area Networks" Dissertation, June 2002, accessed at http://www.s3.kth.se/radio/Publication/Pub2002/Sanchez_Lict2002.pdf.

Sanchez, M., T. Giles, and J. Zander, "CSMA/CA With Beam Forming Antennas in Multi-hop Packet Radio," Proc. Swedish Workshop on Wireless Ad-hoc Networks, March 5–6, 2001.

Sánchez, Ricardo, Joseph Evans, and Gary Minden, "Networking on the Battlefield: Challenges in Highly Dynamic Multi-hop Wireless Networks," IEEE MILCOM, 1999.

Sass, Paul, and Jim Freebersyser, "FCS Communications Technology for the Objective Force," Technical Report, Mitre Corporation, 2002.

Shaaber, Mark, Scott Hedberg, and Troy Wesson, "V Corps: C4ISR Integration AAR," May 2003.

Shen, Chien-Chung, Chavalit Srisathapornphat, Chaiporn Jaikaeo, "Sensor Information Networking Architecture and Applications," *IEEE Personal Communication Magazine*, August 2001.

Sirak, Michael, "U.S. Air Force Targets UAV Bandwidth Problem," *Jane's Defense Weekly*, July 31, 2002.

Spyropoulos, A., and C. Raghavendra, "Energy Efficient Communications in Ad Hoc Networks Using Directional Antennas," in *Proceedings, IEEE Infocom*, 2002.

SRI International, "SRI International and ITT Demonstrate New Technologies that Put Battlefield Information in the Hands of Individual Soldiers," News Release, April 4, 2001, accessed at www.sri.com/news/releases/04-04-01.html.

Srisathapornphat, Chavalit, and Chien-Chung Shen, "Energy Consumption Behavior and Performance of Directional Virtual Carrier Sensing Schemes," IEEE Wireless Communications and Networking Conference (WCNC), New Orleans, LA: March 16–20, 2003. See also http://alfalfa.cis.udel.edu:8080/refs/papers/srisatha03energy.pdf.

Stein, Fred P., "Observations on the Emergence of Network Centric Warfare," Proceedings of the 1998 Command and Control Research and Technology Symposium. Naval Postgraduate School, Monterey, CA, 29 June–1 July 1998, Washington, D.C.: National Defense University, 1998.

Toomey, Christopher, "C4ISR in the Stryker Brigade Combat Teams," *Military Review*, May–June, 2003, pp. 42–46.

Toumpis, S., and A. Goldsmith, "Ad-hoc Network Capacity," *Signals, Systems and Computers*, Conference Record of the Thirty-Fourth Asilomar Conference on, Vol. 2, 2000, pp. 1265–1269.

U.S. Army, "Army RDT&E Budget Item Justification (R-2 Exhibit)," http://www.dtic.mil.descriptivesum/Y2003/Army/0603008A.pdf, 2002.

U.S. Army, *Tactics, Techniques and Procedures for the Enhanced Position Location Reporting System*, FM-24-41, July 1999.

U.S. Army CECOM, "Joint Common Database DII COE Conference," briefing presented April 1999.

U.S. Army CECOM, "Tactical High Speed Data Network," briefing presented March 2002.

U.S. Army CECOM RDEC, Space and Terrestrial Communications Directorate, "Science and Technology Overview, Communications Bandwidth," briefing presented March 2002.

U.S. Army CECOM RDEC, "Multifunctional On-the-Move Secure Adaptive Integrated Communications (MOSAIC) ATD," briefing presented March 2002.

U.S. Army CECOM RDEC, "Brigade Subscriber Node, Networking the Interim Brigade Combat Team," briefing presented March 2002.

U.S. Army CECOM MILSATCOM Project Manager, "Army MILSATCOM Terminal Requirements," briefing presented March 2002.

U.S. Army CECOM OPM TRCS, "Future Bandwidth Requirements for Tactical Radio Products," briefing presented March 2002.

U.S. Army CECOM and The Mitre Corporation, "FCS Communications Networking Architecture," briefing presented March 2002.

U.S. Army TRADOC, Combined Arms Center Army Battle Command Operational Architecture (CACACOA) Version 3.1, ACOA-AM-3.1-Dv1, June 29, 2001.

U.S. Army Signal Center, Brigade Combat Team 1, Version 3.0, March 28, 2001.

U.S. Army TRADOC, *Joint Tactical Radio System Operational Requirements Document*, November 2001.

U.S. Army TRADOC, Migration Plan, *Trojan Spirit II to Warfighter Information Network*, Volume II, August 2001.

U.S. Army TRADOC, WIN-T and JTRS, CSA Information Briefing, February 2002.

U.S Department of Commerce (DOC), "Bush Administration Forges Landmark Plan for Spectrum Allocation," Press Release, July 2002, accessed on September 6, 2002 at http://www.ntia.doc.gov/ntiahome/press/2002/va7232002.htm.

Vaidya, N., "Mobile Ad-Hoc Networks: Routing, MAC and Transport Issues," 2001, accessed at http://www.crhc.uiuc.edu/~nhv on September 2, 2002.

Watts, D. J., *Small Worlds: The Dynamics of Networks Between Order and Randomness*, Princeton University Press, 1999.

Watts, D., and S. Strogatz, "Collective Dynamics of 'Small-World' Networks," *Nature*, Vol. 393, No. 440, 1998.

Wilson, Jeffrey W., "The Importance of Mobility Model Assumptions on Route Discovery, Data Delivery, and Route Maintenance Protocols for Ad-Hoc Mobile Networks," Technical Report, Virginia Polytechnic Institute and State University, December 2001, accessed at http://wilsonjw.tripod.com/wilsonjw011212.pdf.

Yeung, G., M. Takai, and R. Bagrodia, "Integration of an OFDM Radio Model into Qualnct," presented at the ONR Summer 2002 Meeting, http://www.cs.ucla.edu/~gavin.

Yi, Su, Yong Pei, and Shivkumar Kalyanaraman, "On the Capacity Improvement of Ad-hoc Wireless Networks Using Directional Antennas," Proceedings of the Fourth ACM International Conference on Mobile Ad-Hoc Networking and Computing, 2003, pp. 108–116.